Psychology
A Beginner's Guide

D0954806

ONEWORLD BEGINNER'S GUIDES combine an original, inventive, and engaging approach with expert analysis on subjects ranging from art and history to religion and politics, and everything in between. Innovative and affordable, books in the series are perfect for anyone curious about the way the world works and the big ideas of our time.

anarchism
ruth kinna

anti-capitalism
simon tormey

artificial intelligence
blay whitby

the bahá'í faith
moojan momen

the beat generation
christopher gair

biodiversity
john spicer

bioterror & biowarfare
malcolm dando

the brain
a. al-chalabi, m. r. turner & r. s. delamont

christianity
keith ward

cloning
aaron d. levine

criminal psychology
ray bull *et al.*

crimes against humanity
adam jones

daoism
james miller

democracy
david beetham

energy
vaclav smil

evolution
burton s. guttman

evolutionary psychology
r. dunbar, l.barrett & j. lycett

existentialism
thomas e. wartenberg

fair trade
jacqueline decarlo

genetics
a. griffiths, b.guttman, d. suzuki & t. cullis

global terrorism
leonard weinberg

hinduism
klaus k. klostermaier

life in the universe
lewis dartnell

mafia & organized crime
james o. finckenauer

marx
andrew collier

medieval philosophy
sharon m. kaye

NATO
jennifer medcalf

oil
vaclav smil

the palestine–israeli conflict
dan cohn-sherbok & dawoud el-alami

paul
morna d. hooker

philosophy of mind
edward feser

postmodernism
kevin hart

psychology
g. neil martin

quantum physics
alastair i. m. rae

racism
alana lentin

religion
martin forward

the small arms trade
m. schroeder, r. stohl & d. smith

sufism
william c. chittick

SELECTED FORTHCOMING TITLES:

astronomy	feminism	modern slavery
british politics	globalization	philosophy of religion
censorship	history of science	racism
civil liberties	humanism	renaissance art
classics	journalism	romanticism
climate change	literary theory	shakespeare
ethics	middle east	socialism

Psychology
A Beginner's Guide

G. Neil Martin

ONEWORLD
OXFORD

A Oneworld Book

Published by Oneworld Publications 2008

Copyright © G. Neil Martin 2008

ISBN 978–1–85168–602–5

Typeset by Jayvee, Trivandrum, India
Cover design by Simon McFadden
Printed and bound in Great Britain by
TJ International, Padstow, Cornwall

Oneworld Publications
185 Banbury Road
Oxford OX2 7AR
England
www.oneworld-publications.com

Mixed Sources
Product group from well-managed
forests and other controlled sources
www.fsc.org Cert no. SGS-COC-2482
© 1996 Forest Stewardship Council

Learn more about Oneworld. Join our mailing list to
find out about our latest titles and special offers at:

www.oneworld-publications.com

For the University of Aberdeen

The stranger thou hast honoured shall not cease,
In whatsoever ways he rest or roam.
To wish thee noble fortune, fame serene

William Watson (1935)

Contents

Preface

What do psychologists do?

In the sybaritic, shoulder-padded, gel-haired days of the 1980s, I enrolled as an English, Philosophy and Psychology student at an ancient university tucked away on the north-east coast of Scotland. I hadn't intended to study Psychology – my ambition was to become a writer and journalist – but I had to choose a third subject so I asked my mentor (all freshers had one) what he did. He did Psychology. So, I did Psychology.

When I first arrived at university, I had no idea what a psychologist did. In fact, I had no real idea what psychology was and generally confused it with psychiatry – the study and treatment of mental illness. In my second year, I remember reading one thing that has stayed with me. (Many other things have stayed with me too, obviously, or you would probably want a refund, but this one is relevant here.) Sitting on the steps of my lecture theatre, I read the following sentence in my research methods handbook: 'A psychologist', it began, 'has been described as someone who goes to the theatre and watches the audience.'

This was an excellent, well-crafted aphorism, and struck a chord for many reasons.

First, although it was probably a hoary old epigram that had been trotted out to impressionable undergraduates for years, it seemed to sum up psychology's methods succinctly, neatly, wittily, pithily. Second, it crystallised the stereotype of the psychologist as a person who spent most of his – and it was usually a he – time observing and analysing the behaviour of others. Third, it suggested that psychologists made eccentric theatregoers. ('What did you think of his Hamlet/Estragon/Widow-Twanky?' 'No idea, I'm afraid, I was too busy watching aisle two, seat twelve wrestling with a bon bon.')

Fourth, and finally, it was completely wrong.

In this book, I hope to show you how and why, and to give you a flavour of what modern psychology is really about, drawing on classic studies and recent discoveries. Why do we become aggressive? How does the brain allow us to see, hear and feel? Why does prejudice occur? Can we detect lying? What happens when we sleep and does sleep deprivation really impair thinking? Can listening to Mozart improve IQ? How do babies learn to perceive and think? Are there basic emotions and, if so, what are they? Why do we become mentally ill? Does psychotherapy work? Do we really stand by as others suffer? Can personality and intelligence be measured? Why do we claim to remember things that didn't happen? How does persuasion work? Why do we forget? Do we prefer certain body types and, if so, why? Is it better to forgive and forget? Can we reduce obesity and cigarette smoking? Is being physically attractive an advantage? Some tentative answers to these questions can be found in the following pages.

A book of this size, however, can only offer a (hopefully mesmerising) glimpse of the science of behaviour – and psychologists, like all scientists, inevitably quarrel about the right answers to all of these questions and others. The further reading at the end of each chapter will lead you to further sources of information.

If you have any comments on what you've read, I'd be delighted to hear from you (email me at: n.martin@mdx.ac.uk; URL: www.mdx.ac.uk/hssc/staff/profiles/academic/martinn.asp).

My thanks go to Dr Nicky Brunswick for reading through

the first draft of the manuscript, and Marsha Filion for commissioning the book you're holding, for her enthusiasm and tenacity in seeing it through, and for her impeccable taste in patisserie.

So, from this point on, leave any prejudices and assumptions you might have right here. The reality is guaranteed to be a lot more interesting. Enjoy the journey.

(Shoulder-pads not essential.)

G. Neil Martin

Illustrations

1

What is psychology?

Like reality television, politicians, art and Paris Hilton, everybody seems to have an opinion about psychology and what it means. We think we understand people well, that we can predict their behaviour – say that person X has such-and-such a personality, that person B would 'never do something like that' or 'does not suffer fools gladly'. Even when people's behaviour falls short of our predictions, we still cling onto our beliefs about the way that others behave. In a sense, we behave like lay scientists (but sometimes very bad ones): we create predictions or hypotheses ('Sarah is the life and soul of the party') that are supported by evidence ('Sarah engages in raucous karaoke and customarily drinks everyone under the table'). If these predictions are not supported, however, we sometimes feel that it is not the hypothesis that is at fault (after all, *we* can't be wrong) but the subject of the testing (Sarah is usually the life and soul of the party but something must have happened today to make her unwilling to belt out Aqua on the karaoke machine). That Sarah may be erecting a sociable, extravert facade because she is a lonely person, ravaged by self-doubt and is trying to cope with her pain through drink and partying isn't normally considered. Psychologists try and see beyond the obvious.

Psychology has been defined in many ways but the most succinct is: the scientific study of human and non-human behaviour. The word comes from the Greek, *psukhe*, meaning 'breath' or 'soul', and *logos*, meaning 'word' or 'reason', and its subject matter can range from the physiological and neural (heart rate, say, or the activation of various parts of the brain) to the overtly, physically observable (responding to a stimulus, using a computer keyboard or responding to other people) to the indirectly observable (memory processes, reasoning, personality, emotion).

The important part of the definition is 'scientific' because psychologists approach the study of behaviour in a specific way. They construct hypotheses (ideas about the world that can be tested) and then create experiments in which these ideas are tested. If the experiment supports the hypothesis, all well and good – the hypothesis is probably correct. If not, the hypothesis needs to be modified. (Evidence in a well-conducted experiment cannot be ignored, even if you do not like the conclusion.) Psychology occupies an interesting position in the science hierarchy. A recent study by Dean Simonton in the USA compared the scientific status of psychology, biology, physics, and sociology. Simonton looked at the number of theories and laws mentioned in introductory texts, the number of graphs in journal articles, the impact of young researchers, perceived difficulty of the subject, as well as factors such as 'lecture disfluency' (the number of *ums* and *ahs* in lectures – these are more common in less structured and factual disciplines). Taking all these into account, psychology was ranked alongside biology and between physics, which was top of the hierarchy, and sociology, which was at the bottom.

Let's apply the scientific method to a potentially important issue. Imagine you want to test the hypothesis that cannabis use makes you an inattentive or dangerous driver. A psychologist might set up an experiment in which randomly chosen, experienced men and women drivers in a given age range receive different doses of cannabis (or none, or a substance they think is cannabis but isn't – a placebo) while aspects of their driving performance (such as speed, attention, lane drifting, braking, etc.) is assessed in a driving simulator, over a period of time. The psychologist's approach to understanding behaviour, as this fairly common example shows, is different – more complex and methodical – to that of the layperson (although, in fairness, the layperson is probably not supported by a multi-million pound university laboratory, nor has access to a huge sample of participants, plentiful computing and statistics software, nor has the time to do this).

This approach means that much of what is discovered can be counter-intuitive or contradicts 'common-sense'. According to the poet Samuel Taylor Coleridge, 'common sense in an uncommon degree is what the rest of the world calls wisdom'. Common-sense answers in psychology, however, tend to be the wrong ones. Probably the greatest British psychologist of the twentieth century, Hans J. Eysenck in his 1957 book, *Sense and Nonsense in Psychology*, summed it up in this way:

> It appears to be an almost universal belief that anyone is competent to discuss psychological problems, whether he or she has taken the trouble to study the subject or not, and that while everybody's opinion is of equal value, that of the professional psychologist must be excluded at all costs because he might spoil the fun by producing some facts which would completely upset the speculation and the wonderful dream castles so laboriously constructed by the layman.

Consider lying, for example. A standard policing manual, as well as a survey conducted by the Global Deception Research Team in 2006, considered 'averting gaze' to be the best clue to a person's guilt/deception. Other clues were placing the hand over the mouth or eyes and playing with hair. Research, however, has revealed very different behaviours to be better predictors of mendacity. In fact, the two best predictors of lying (at least, according to recent studies) are described in chapter 9.

You can probably tell where this line of thinking is going, but take a look at the following statements. Which do you think are true and which are false?

- A person with schizophrenia has a split-personality.
- Women are more likely to conform than are men.
- When making decisions, committees tend to be more conservative than individuals.
- Dangerous riots are more likely to occur in very high temperatures (e.g. 30 degrees Celsius).
- The more motivated you are, the better able you are to solve complex problems.
- A mild electric shock directly administered to the brain leads to pain and neural tissue destruction.
- People who threaten to commit suicide rarely do.
- We only use ten per cent of our brain.
- Astrology is a good predictor of personality.
- When feeding infants, 'breast is best' in terms of psychological development.
- Traffic accidents and murders are more likely to occur when the moon is full.
- The saying 'opposites attract' in romantic relationships is generally true.
- Psychology and psychoanalysis are the same.

If you thought that all of these were *false* – well done! Most research indicates that all of these statements are untrue (and the first and last statements are simply factually inaccurate). If you thought the majority of them were true, you have made a common-sense mistake. Don't worry – you're in good company. Studies of undergraduates find that even psychology students sometimes get at most only fifty per cent of answers right when asked questions about psychological research where the obvious answer, the common-sense one, is the wrong one. Sociology students perform even worse. And engineering students clearly live on some well-oiled planet of their own. This little exercise shows that common sense is not an entirely accurate predictor of findings in psychology.

What do psychologists do?

Nowadays, hardly any person calls him or herself a psychologist. The breadth of the subject matter in psychology means that psychologists specialise in a specific field and are known by a specialism – they may study memory, say, or the workings of the brain or the senses, or how people interact with each other. In these examples, they would be called cognitive psychologists, neuropsychologists/biological psychologists and social psychologists, respectively. The different branches of psychology (and, by extension, the different types of psychologist) are described in table 1.

Psychologists conduct experiments, advise on health and educational issues and on better ways of working for local and national government, help treat and diagnose people with psychological disorders, are involved in assessment of personality and intelligence (children's and adults'), teach and undertake research. They work in universities, industry, commerce, hospitals, advertising, schools – any arena where an understanding of behaviour can be applied or studied. Psychologists usually have a first university degree in psychology or a related subject, a postgraduate research degree such as an MSc and a higher degree or doctorate (PhD). They are different to psychiatrists, who hold medical degrees and specialise in mental illness/disorders (and can, therefore, prescribe medication). The work of psychiatrists is similar to that of clinical psychologists, except that the former have a medical degree and can prescribe medication and the latter a postgraduate doctorate in clinical psychology (called a DClinPsy).

Psychotherapists can be psychologists but you do not need to be a psychologist to be a psychotherapist. A psychotherapist aims to understand and treat mental distress from a particular theoretical/ideological standpoint. Psychotherapy is usually called the 'talking cure' (although it rarely cures) because it primarily involves talking through a person's problem, but some forms are

Table 1 The major branches of psychology

Branch	Subject of study
Psychobiology/Biological psychology	Biological basis of behaviour
Psychophysiology	Psychophysiological responses such as heart rate, galvanic skin response and brain electrical activity
Neuropsychology	Relationship between brain activity/ structure and function
Comparative psychology	Behaviour of species in terms of evolution and adaptation
Ethology	Animal behaviour in natural environments
Sociobiology	Social behaviour in terms of biological inheritance and evolution
Behaviour genetics	Degree of influence of genetics and environment on psychological factors
Cognitive psychology	Mental processes and complex behaviour
Cognitive neuroscience	Brain's involvement in mental processes
Developmental psychology	Physical, cognitive, social and emotional development from birth to senescence
Social psychology	Individuals' and groups' behaviour
Individual differences	Temperament and characteristics of individuals and their effects on behaviour
Cross-cultural psychology	Impact of culture on behaviour
Cultural psychology	Variability of behaviour within cultures
Forensic/criminological psychology	Behaviour in the context of crime and the law
Clinical psychology	Causes and treatment of mental disorder
Health psychology	Impact of lifestyle and stress on health and illness
Educational psychology	Social, cognitive and emotional development of children in the context of schooling

much more methodical and involve changing the client's way of thinking and behaviour, not just listening to his/her outpouring. Cognitive behavioural therapy (CBT), for example, which has been used to treat certain forms of depression successfully, involves getting the patient to think differently about how he/she thinks (why he/she thinks negatively) and to make explicit plans to change the way he/she behaves. There is even evidence to suggest that CBT can help unemployed people find work (because of its emphasis on doing, as well as thinking). There are hundreds of different types of psychotherapy and we'll return to the most reputable in the last chapter.

Psychoanalysis, probably the name most commonly confused with psychology (never confuse the two when talking to a proper psychologist – it won't be a happy conversation), has little to do with modern scientific psychology. It takes the thought and work of early twentieth-century physicians such as Sigmund Freud, Carl Jung, Alfred Adler and Karen Horney, and applies it to understanding and managing emotional and behavioural problems. Most of these theories describe the workings of the 'unconscious' which is argued to influence our conscious life. Few psychologists take psychoanalysis seriously. It is also a very difficult field to which to apply scientific standards because some parts are untestable. If, for example, you admit that your unusual behaviour is due to some traumatic event in your childhood, that fits the theory. If you do not, it still fits the theory because you are simply repressing the memory of the event that caused your mental turmoil. We'll come back to Freud and colleagues in the chapter on individual differences.

Ideas and schools of thought in psychology

Psychology likes to regard itself as a young science and the regard is not unfounded. The first person to call himself a psychologist was still living in 1920; the first modern laboratory in experimental psychology was set up in 1878, in Germany; even at the beginning of the twentieth century, some universities would offer courses in 'mental philosophy' (rather than what we'd now call psychology). The discipline has, therefore, travelled phenomenally quickly in a short space of time. But it is not only psychologists who think about psychological issues. The history of psychology goes beyond 1878, and its historical milestones and influences have shaped the way the discipline has developed.

Like all of the sciences, psychology has its roots in philosophy and the schools of philosophical thought with which it has been most closely associated are animism, dualism, empiricism, idealism, and materialism. In short, this is what each contributed.

Animism – a primitive philosophy (from the Latin *animare*, 'to enliven, endow with soul') in which animate and inanimate objects were thought to have a spirit that guided movement. Because bodily movement was thought to be controlled by the mind or spirit, so were other moving objects such as the sun and moon (and even a falling rock). Of historical interest now, psychologically it is interesting because within it is the notion that we attribute internal causes to external events (think of attributing a person's behaviour to 'will power'). Inference is one thing, however, objectively observing and measuring behaviour/activity, as the scientific method dictates, is another.

Dualism – famously proposed by the French mathematician René Descartes (1569–1650), this approach argued that reality could be divided into two distinct entities, the mind or 'thinking things', and matter or 'extended things' (hence, dual-ism; it is also called Cartesian dualism). Extended things such as physical bodies cannot think and the mind cannot be made of matter. Descartes, the father of modern philosophy (and, some would say, psychology, too), was an acute observer of behaviour – he described movements that were not under conscious control, for example (reflexes). The perception of a hot flame did not require the considered involvement of the mind – the body would reflexively withdraw. A person does not intend to recoil from the heat and so the response is mechanical, involuntary (essentially, a series of muscle contractions).

Descartes, however, suggested that mind and matter can interact (this was called interactionism), a departure from thinkers such as Plato who thought that the two entities were separate but that the mind could influence the body but not vice versa (the puppet could not control the puppet master). Other philosophers disagreed with Descartes too, arguing, in Spinoza's case, that mind and matter were different aspects of the same entity in the same way that a line can be convex or concave. Descartes's thinking was influenced, in part, by seeing mechanical moving statues at the Royal Gardens as a child – pressing on a plate would make one of the statues move. This coloured his mechanical view of how the world worked. Descartes influenced two later, very different schools of thought in psychology: introspectionism and behaviourism.

Empiricism – the pursuit of truth through observation and experience, this was a seventeenth-century idea proposed by English philosopher, John Locke (1632–1704). Some thinkers at the time argued that ability and ideas were innate; Locke argued that ideas were learned through experience: the mind was a tabula rasa (a tablet of clay) onto which experience would create its impressions. The idea was developed in more detail by the Scottish philosopher, David Hume (1711–1776). He proposed a philosophy whereby ideas could be reduced to observable material (positivism). He also developed the doctrine of association – the notion that a stimulus or idea can trigger associations to other stimuli/ideas. Events paired often enough become a habit. If you learn that flicking a switch will turn the light on, that becomes a habit learned.

Materialism – the notion that reality can only be understood by understanding the physical world (of which the mind is a part). Proposed by the Scottish philosopher James Mill (1773–1836), this interpretation contrasted with Descartes's dualism because it did not regard the mind as, literally, immaterial.

The birth of modern psychology

At this point in history, in a small town in Germany, psychology begins to release itself from the umbilical cord of philosophy. The midwife was Wilhelm Wundt (1832–1920), the first man to call himself a psychologist, who set up the first laboratory in psychology at Leipzig and authored the first psychology textbook. The development of experimental psychology was helped by the intellectual climate in Germany – the experimental study of physiology, for example, had become well established there. Wundt dedicated his laboratory to the experimental study of psychological processes and developed a school of thought (the first in psychology) called structuralism in which the mind was conceived as comprising elements of consciousness such as ideas and thoughts; these were like the chemical table of elements and could be similarly arranged. Trained observers would describe their own experiences, especially visual and auditory sensations (introspectionism), as they participated in reaction time studies, amongst others. Although important at the time, the school died out at the beginning of the twentieth century when one of introspectionism's fiercest critics, the American John B. Watson, dismissed the subjective, unscientific nature of introspections and unleashed one of psychology's most powerful schools of thought, which we'll return to in a short while.

Before that, however, but still in the USA, another school of thought was making itself felt. The functionalism of the greatest American psychologist, William James, and his colleague James Angell sought to find out how processes such as learning and perception worked (hence, function), rather than studying mental structure. The emphasis was on observable behaviour, not mental events.

Functionalism was informed by Darwin's thoughts on the origins of species and evolution: behaviours, like physical material, evolved. Darwin's cousin, Sir Francis Galton, also made an important contribution to psychology by founding the discipline of psychometrics (assessment of personality and ability) and establishing the Anthropometric Laboratory at University College London in 1884 where intelligence testing was born. (Galton polymathically invented the term correlation, constructed the first weather maps of Britain, invented finger-printing and was the first person to describe the anticyclone.) He was one of the first to study the heritability of psychological variables, arguing that eminent fathers bred eminent sons who bred further, eminent offspring. Of course, eminence might just as well be determined by environment (and Galton did not use a comparison group of non-eminent men, as any good study would have) but Galton's approach was innovative in suggesting that psychological traits could be inherited.

As Wundt was developing his experimental manifesto in Leipzig, in Vienna, a physician was embarking on an altogether different approach to understanding behaviour, one which has had more effect on the perception of psychology than any other. Although his original research was rooted in biology and medicine, Sigmund Freud (1856–1939) constructed a theory of personality (psychodynamic theory), based on patient observation rather than experiment, and which emphasised the role of the unconscious in behaviour. Freud's approach, like Wundt's, featured structures, but these were the id, ego and superego. We'll look at these in more depth in the individual differences chapter.

Meanwhile, in the USA, a juggernaut was revving. Behaviourism – the study of observable behaviour – was conceived as a violent reaction to introspectionism. Behaviourists believed that mental events were unobservable and, therefore, could not be studied. They went further: mental life was of no interest at all (because we couldn't study it properly). Ivan Pavlov, a Russian physiologist and the unwitting progenitor of behaviourism, contributed powerfully to this school by demonstrating that it was possible to condition behaviour without recourse to mental life or introspectionism. Famously, Pavlov discovered that hungry dogs were capable of learning that two previously unrelated stimuli could become associated. When presented with food, the dogs would salivate; when Pavlov rang a bell, they would not. If the bell was paired with food often enough, however, the subsequent sound of the bell alone led to salivation. The dogs had learned an association between the bell and the appearance of food, hence the salivation. Through experience, the organism responded to a stimulus which it had previously not responded to.

This was developed at the human level by John B. Watson and crystallised in Watson's behaviourist manifesto, *Psychology from the Standpoint of the Behaviourist*, published in 1919. Rejecting introspectionism completely, Watson, a convincing and charismatic psychologist, argued that psychology was a purely objective experimental branch of natural science. Watson's subject matter was observable behaviour – people and animals' responses to stimuli. His approach has been absorbed into mainstream psychology so seamlessly that behaviourism does not exist as a school any more. There will be more on Watson's experiments in the chapter on learning.

The period between 1930 and 1960 saw behaviourism developing in a more radical direction and the man who made the most significant, perhaps most important, contribution to this period was Burrhus Frederick Skinner (1904–1990). A behaviourist, Skinner developed a model of behaviour based on stimulus and response, and on reinforcement of behaviour especially. In the most influential studies ever conducted in learning, he found that pigeons could be trained to change their behaviour depending on the reinforcement they were given. They would receive food only if they behaved in a particular way such as pressing a lever either once or four times, for example: the pigeons learned to press the lever only once or four times to receive food. This became known as operant – or instrumental – conditioning because the organism had to 'operate' on the environment. Humans and animals were machines that behaved in lawful ways: they were empty organisms. The mind or mental operations were irrelevant. We'll return to operant conditioning in more detail in chapter 4.

The cognitive and biological revolutions

Another new school emerged in the 1960s – the decade of the so-called cognitive revolution – that placed more emphasis on how we and other organisms process information delivered to the brain via the senses. The computer was adopted as the model of how the brain (or mind) worked. Another revolution – the biological revolution – also influenced psychology and had its origins in the nineteenth century, e.g. it was observed that cells in the brain communicated via electrical impulses, regardless of whether the impulse was carrying information about what the eye saw or the ear heard.

In the middle of the nineteenth century, two reports changed the way in which we understood how the brain processed one of the most distinctive human behaviours: speech. The French surgeon, Pierre Paul Broca (1824–1880), described a patient called 'Tan' (his real name was Leborgne, but all he could utter was 'Tan'). Tan had suffered a stroke and was unable to produce fluent speech. At autopsy, Broca discovered a small, egg-shaped cavity on the left side of the front of Tan's brain. This, Broca reasoned, was the centre for speech – it is now known as Broca's area and the disorder seen in Tan is known as Broca's aphasia. Another group of patients reported by Carl Wernicke had the opposite problem – they could speak but not comprehend speech. Damage here was to an area near that damaged in Tan, an area now called Wernicke's area; the condition is called Wernicke's aphasia. This, Wernicke reasoned, was where the brain processed the sounds of speech to make a coherent, meaningful word or sentence. We now know that these conclusions are a little too crude – to produce severe inability to speak, damage needs to be more extensive than that seen in Tan. But, in general, they stand. These patients also represent psychology's first real, and most famous, single-case studies. You'll find many others in this book, such as Phineas Gage whose personality and social behaviour changed following brain damage, and HM whose brain surgery led to an inability to learn new memories.

Two other milestones are important. In 1870, two scientists, Gustav Fritsch and Eduard Hitzig, demonstrated, experimentally and for the first time, that a function or behaviour was localised in the brain – that is, a part of the brain was responsible for a specific function or behaviour. They found that electrically stimulating different parts of a dog's brain led to movements in different parts of the animal's body. Unlike the case studies above, which were not experimental, but correlational (brain injury was reasoned to lead to a language problem), this was the first to stimulate the brain experimentally and observe the consequences.

A second milestone, but not one that is now taken seriously, was reached by Gall and Spurzheim in the nineteenth century. They reasoned that areas of the brain that were specialised for a function – morality, say, or mathematics – would become overactive. This overactivity would lead to an indentation in the skull above it. The study was called anatomical personology or phrenology. The theory was ludicrous and was quickly disproved when one of phrenology's fiercest critics presented the brain of a criminal imbecile to Gall and Spurzheim – the cadaver exhibited bumps that would have made him a mathematical genius. But the general thrust contained the germ of modern localisation of function: the notion that different regions of the brain undertake different functions.

Psychologists still study people with brain injury – the invaluable data they provide about the role of the brain in functional impairment could not be obtained in any other way. Modern psychology, however, also harnesses the majestic power of the brain imager. These machines allow researchers to measure and picture brain structure and activation, based on specific physiological processes such as blood flow or oxygen consumption. The most well known are Magnetic Resonance Imaging, functional Magnetic Resonance Imaging, and Positron Emission Tomography and they have been used to study almost every behaviour imaginable – from face perception to speaking, to reading, to smelling and tasting, to inferring the motivation of others, to experiencing emotion, to making moral decisions, to being in love, to having an erection. We'll find out more about them, and their advantages and disadvantages, in the next chapter.

How psychologists study behaviour

As you saw earlier, psychologists adopt the scientific method because it is the best way of gaining knowledge. They do this in three general ways. They can conduct naturalistic studies (as Darwin did when he took his Voyage on the Beagle, or as the Swiss developmental psychologist Jean Piaget did when he observed his children's play and cognitive development);

correlational studies, where associations are made between two or more measured factors (e.g. the relationship between personality and intelligence or physical beauty and intelligence); and experiments. Unlike the other two methods, experiments do not simply measure – they make things happen and, normally, an experimenter will follow five steps when conducting an experiment:

1. Identify a problem and draw cause-and-effect inferences
2. Design the experiment
3. Conduct the experiment
4. Examine the data to see if hypotheses are supported
5. Communicate the results

Before you read the rest of the book, it is useful to become familiar with the terms commonly used in this process. Here are some of the most widely used:

Hypothesis: a statement or prediction made in a study, usually about a cause-and-effect relationship between two events

Theory: a set of statements to explain a phenomenon; hypotheses are derived from theory

Quantitative research: experiments studying quantifiable behaviour or events, e.g. intelligence test scores, reaction time, heart rate, level of hormones produced

Control: a group in an experiment that acts as a comparison because it is unaffected by the experiment itself

Experimental group: the group in an experiment which is directly affected by the experiment, e.g. the group that receives a drug, or completes a test under certain conditions

Independent/between-groups design: the groups in the experiment are not the same, e.g. one group may take drug A, a second drug B – neither takes both

Within groups/repeated measures design: groups are exposed to all conditions of the experiment, e.g. in an experiment to see whether people recognise English words faster than they do pseudo-words or non-words, all participants are exposed to each type of word

Variable: things which have a value but can vary; in experiments these are what psychologists manipulate, e.g. lighting conditions, type of word, anxiety level, IQ score, even sex

Independent variable: the directly manipulated factor in the experiment, e.g. a psychologist might manipulate mood by having participants recall sad or happy memories; the effect of mood on, say, creativity can then be measured; mood, here, is the independent variable

Dependent variable: the variable that is measured. In the previous example, creative output

Validity: does a study measure what it claims to study? Two well-known examples of validity failure are Clever Hans and the Barnum Effect (more on this below)

Reliability: does a study consistently measure what it claims to measure? Measurement of adult height is fairly reliable (this will not change from one week to the other); measuring people's academic ability might be less reliable

Qualitative research: very different from quantitative research, this studies meaning and context in a person's behaviour (such as their speech or writing); the emphasis is on the individual's experience, reactions and feelings, as revealed in their words

When validity fails: horses and circuses

You can learn about psychology in the oddest of places and from the oddest of things. A horse, for example. Clever Hans is famous in the psychology literature, not for any equine prowess but for highlighting the importance of questioning what you see and hear. Hans was a horse who could, apparently, perform extraordinary feats of mind-reading. People would give Hans's owner a question to ask him – such as 'what is 2 + 3?' – and the horse would, in an act that staggered onlookers, tap out the correct answer with his hoof. The wonder horse so captivated German society that, in 1904, a commission was formed to study this brilliant mind-reading nag. It concluded that the horse could not have been responding to external clues from the people around him and that it could, indeed, be the Derren Brown of the stable.

A psychologist on the commission, however, was more sceptical and asked a graduate student to look into this. The student suggested putting blinkers on the horse so that it could not act on any external visual cue. When this was done, Hans's remarkable powers deserted him. What Hans was supremely adept at was reading others' body language, sometimes subtle physical cues.

The example of Clever Hans is a lesson in scepticism – questioning what seems obvious or extraordinary and eliminating possible reasons for a phenomenon that is witnessed.

Let's continue the theme, by visiting the circus, specifically the Barnum effect. Take a look at the following statements and indicate truthfully which you think best sum you up. There is no minimum number to choose – you can pick as many as you like.

- You are the type of person who has a tendency to be critical of yourself.
- You have a great need for other people to like and admire you but you pride yourself on being an independent thinker and do not accept others' statements without satisfactory proof.
- You have a great deal of unused capacity which you have not turned to your advantage.
- While you have some personality weaknesses, you are generally able to compensate for them.

- You prefer a certain amount of change and variety and become dissatisfied when hemmed in by restrictions and limitations.

Did you find that most of these statements described you? You probably did, because these statements could apply to just about anyone. This is called the Barnum effect, named after the great circus showman P.T. Barnum who believed that there was a 'sucker born every minute' and believed that his entertainment provided a little bit of something for everybody. It is exploited ruthlessly, if toothlessly, by astrologers and the like who give predictions so vague and general that their prognostications could apply to all star-signs. (If there's anything we Aquarians hate, it's over-generalisation.) Psychologists have tested the strength of this effect in various contexts and it is strong, even in presumably intelligent people like undergraduates and personnel managers. In an unusual experiment, Adrian Furnham at UCL asked participants to provide a lock of their hair for 'trichological analysis' – the participants would be given feedback on their health based on the sample some time later. The participants were actually given twenty-four bogus, bland statements. Some of these included: 'your diet, while adequate, would benefit from an increase in fruit and vegetables', 'you are probably hairier than most other people of your age and sex' and 'you occasionally get a craving for certain foods'. Most participants thought the statements they were given were very accurate, even though they were completely made up.

In the next chapters, you'll see how the methods and critical approach described here have been applied to various behaviours – from brain activity to social development and mental health.

2

The nervous system: biological psychology in action

In a lecture I give to students on our MSc in forensic psychology course, I show a slide of a headline from a national newspaper: 'Scans spot killer babies', it shouts alarmingly. The headline illustrates two things: neuroimaging techniques (which were only developed in the past twenty years) have afforded scientists a tremendous opportunity to investigate the relationship between behaviour and the brain in a way that was inconceivable thirty years ago. Second, it illustrates how you can over-egg the neuroimaging pudding. These colourful, innovative techniques can do many things but there are some things they can't do. Many claims have been made for brain scanning techniques – detecting liars, finding the morality centre in the brain, spotting killer babies ... amongst other fantastical ambitions ('The brain scan that can read people's intentions,' bellowed *The Guardian's* front page in February 2007). Of course, they can't do any of these things (yet) but they have provided a monumental body of data on how the brain behaves when it engages in all sorts of functions, from language production and comprehension, to emotion, to sensation and perception and many, many others. Some of these techniques and what they do are described later. The brain, according to Woody Allen, was his second favourite organ. The next section describes the elements of the second which help him think about his first.

The brain: a quick tour

All behaviour arises from the operation of the brain. For this reason, psychologists have studied its structure and function extensively. The brain (and the spinal cord leading from it) is part of the nervous system called the central nervous system (CNS). All of the nerves outside the CNS are part of the peripheral nervous system: these connect the CNS with information that comes from the body's sense organs, muscles and glands. The brain, in adult humans, is an unflattering porridge-coloured 1400g lump of wobbling tissue. This lump, however, allows us to do everything described in this book.

The brain is well protected, not only by the skull but also by fluid (cerebrospinal fluid) and several layers of protective membrane called meninges. It has two halves (called cerebral hemispheres) connected by a thick band of white tissue called the corpus callosum – when this is surgically severed, some patients ('split-brain' patients) behave as if they had two brains because the two hemispheres are unable to communicate with each other.

The outer covering of the brain is called the cortex ('bark') and has a convoluted appearance because it is folded and made up of fissures (grooves), sulci (smaller grooves) and gyri (bulges), which give the brain a wrinkled appearance. This allows the brain to maximise its surface area within the skull: imagine trying to fit a sheet of A4 paper into a matchbox. You wouldn't be able to do this unless you folded or scrunched the paper to get it to fit inside. This is what happens within the skull as the brain develops. The more complex the organism, the more wrinkled the cortex. This part of the brain is responsible for our thoughts, emotions, perceptions and other behaviours, and is the most recently developed (the youngest part of your brain – in terms of evolution – is the front part). You can see this and other CNS structures in figure 1.

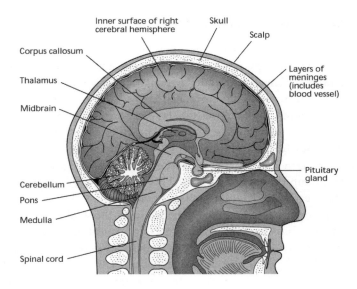

Figure 1 Structures of the human Central Nervous System

The cortex is also known as the cerebrum; there is another structure at the back and slightly underneath the brain which looks like a little brain, called the cerebellum. This is involved in posture and maintaining balance, amongst other things.

From the back of the brain extend the pons and medulla oblongata, or brain stem. The brain's cranial nerves originate here – there are twelve of these conveying information about the senses and muscles to the rest of the brain. The trigeminal nerve, the largest, responds to chemical stimulation: crying to a peeling onion or the whack of the smell of ammonia is due to stimulation of the trigeminus. Behaviours such as chewing are allowed because the command to chew is communicated via a cranial nerve. Speech muscles, eye muscles and tongue movement are also controlled by the cranial nerves.

Brain cells

The brain comprises between 10 billion and 100 billion nerve cells (neurons) and just as many supporting cells (or glial cells, which assist neurons). We are born with all of the neurons we will ever have; in fact, after birth there is a massive suicide of cells, a pruning that continues through adulthood. Neurons communicate via electrical currents and chemicals. A neuron has at least one nerve fibre, an axon, which looks a bit like a cable and is milky coloured because it is covered in a sheath of substance called myelin. This carries messages to other cells where it terminates in a synapse, the point of connection between the end of an axon and another cell. A synapse can excite (stimulate another cell) or inhibit (stop another cell from behaving in a particular way).

The neuron also has processes extending from it called dendrites. These receive messages from other cells. At the end of an axon there are 'terminal buttons' which synapse onto other cells: these buttons release substances called neurotransmitters (there are various types) which influence behaviour and are taken up by receiving cells. Any chemical not used is either cleared away by supporting cells or taken back up by the releasing nerve (a process called reuptake). Neurotransmitters are essential to the functioning of the brain. In depression, for example, there is a reduction in the neurotransmitter serotonin, which anti-depressant medication seeks to restore; in Parkinson's disease, a serious motor disorder in which the patient makes uncontrollable movements, there is excess production of another neurotransmitter, dopamine, which drugs such as L-DOPA inhibit. Both neurotransmitters contribute to a huge variety of behaviours.

The release of the neurotransmitter is caused by an electrical signal coming down the axon. This is called the action potential (the firing of an axon). The gaps in the parts of the axon that are not myelinated allow the electrical impulse to travel more quickly – it can jump from one myelin-covered portion to the next. In disorders such as multiple sclerosis, the axon is not myelinated at all, which makes the impulse either very slow or non-existent. The way in which cells communicate is fantastically complex and the above description does not even begin to scratch the surface – but you can find more on this in the further reading section.

Areas of the brain and what they do

Two brains look very much alike but, anatomically, they are very different on close inspection. The cortex is traditionally divided into four portions, called lobes: these are the frontal (the largest, covering about one-third of the cortex), temporal, parietal and occipital lobes. They're so-called, not for some important psychological reason, but after the part of the skull above them. It so happens, however, that each lobe does have specific functions which others have little or no involvement in. Take a look at figure 2 to see the location of each lobe.

The idea that a function or behaviour is the responsibility of a specific part of the brain is called localisation of function. If the function is localised on one side of the brain, it is said to be lateralised (if it is localised in a region in both hemispheres, it is bilateral). Here are some of the functions associated with each lobe:

Occipital lobe
Perceiving and manipulating visual information
Perceiving objects and faces
Mental imagery

Temporal lobe
Recognising spoken words
Comprehending language

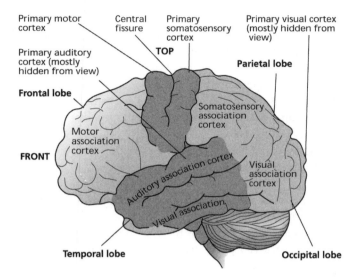

Figure 2 The lobes of the brain

Retrieving general knowledge
Encoding autobiographical memories
Formation memories
Processing sounds and music
Reading Braille

Parietal lobe

Attention
Perceiving and understanding spatial relations
Imagery
Skill learning
Reaching
Memory retrieval
Arithmetical ability
Somatosensation (sense of touch)

Frontal lobe
>   Working memory (the ability to retain information in the
>   short term while executing a simultaneous act or thought)
>   Sustaining attention
>   Inhibiting inappropriate emotions
>   Initiating, planning, and sequencing movements
>   Detecting, and discriminating between, smells
>   Understanding jokes
>   Being aware of others' intentions and thoughts
>   Experiencing positive and negative emotion

Within the lobes are the areas of cortex responsible for perception – hearing, smelling, tasting, touching, and seeing. When the senses project to the brain, it is these areas that make sense of the senses – the eye is a good example because the information it senses goes through various routes, regions, and structures. Ultimately, it ends up in the part of the brain called the primary visual cortex, which makes sense of visual sense impressions. It understands whether an object was moving, what colour it was, how sharply it was seen, and so on. The primary auditory cortex does the same job for sound, the primary motor cortex for movement, and the somatosensory cortex for touch. The more complex the movement created by a body part (the fingers or the lips during speech, for example), the greater the amount of cortex dedicated to it, as figure 3a shows.

The motor cortex is also 'crossed' – the right side of the brain is primarily responsible for left body side movement and the left hemisphere, the right side (the same is also the case for vision – information from the left visual field goes to the right hemisphere). There is some evidence of crossing in the auditory system, too, but it also sends projections to the hemisphere on the same side as the receiving ear. There are secondary (association) cortices which receive information from the primary areas. You can see the primary and secondary cortices in figures 3a and

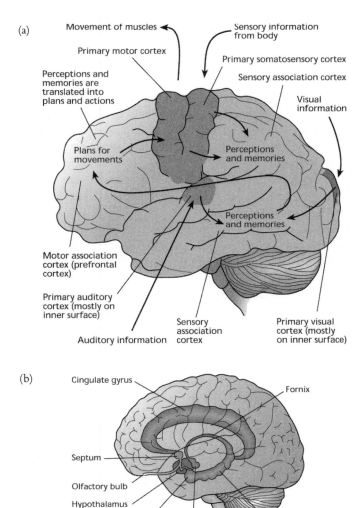

(a)

Movement of muscles ◄

Sensory information from body

Primary motor cortex

Primary somatosensory cortex

Perceptions and memories are translated into plans and actions

Sensory association cortex

Visual information

Plans for movements

Perceptions and memories

Perceptions and memories

Motor association cortex (prefrontal cortex)

Primary auditory cortex (mostly on inner surface)

Sensory association cortex

Primary visual cortex (mostly on inner surface)

Auditory information

(b)

Cingulate gyrus

Fornix

Septum

Olfactory bulb

Hypothalamus

Amygdala

Mammillary body

Hippocampus

Figure 3 (a) Areas of the cortex devoted to movement; (b) Parts of the sub-cortex/limbic system

3b. Curiously, there is a great deal of overlap between the areas involved in actual visual perception and movement and those involved in imagining visual images and movement (such as imagining using a pen).

Beneath the cortex is an area collectively known as the subcortex. This comprises some of the brain's oldest structures – in terms of evolution, the brain stem and these structures were the first to develop. Their age, therefore, suggests that their function is 'primitive' and, in a sense, it is – they regulate hunger, thirst, eating, drinking, fear, movement and so on. Some of the most important of these structures and what they do (amongst other things) are:

The *thalamus* (Greek for inner chamber) – receives sensory information and integrates it; also acts as a kind of sensory relay station for the brain, processing information before sending it to the cortex.

The *hypothalamus* – located below the thalamus (hence the name), this is a small region involved in detecting changes in the body's physiology, which monitors aspects of blood as it goes through the brain. It controls a small structure, the pituitary gland, which produces hormones – chemicals that stimulate the body to do things, a little like neurotransmitters do but over much longer distances. It also controls the autonomic nervous system (ANS) – the part of the nervous system that control glands and internal organs. The sympathetic branch of the ANS directs activities that involve expending energy – increasing blood flow to muscles to prepare them for action, such as running, making the heart contract more quickly, dilating pupils, ejaculating/orgasming; the parasympathetic branch controls less overtly active processes, such as food digestion, pupil constriction, erection/vaginal lubrication.

The *basal ganglia* – a collection of nuclei, involved in movement amongst other behaviours (they are directly affected in Parkinson's Disease and surgery used to treat Parkinson's targets these structures specifically).

The limbic system – a short-hand term for a collection of subcortical structures, two of the most important being the amygdala and the hippocampus. The amygdala has a role in monitoring the environment for threat or negative events, recognising fear and controlling short-term physiological processes involved in fighting or fleeing. The hippocampus is important for the formation of memories – people with hippocampal damage fail to learn new things. It also allows, with other brain regions, spatial navigation (as will be seen in chapter 4). You can see the location of some of these in figure 3b.

Studying the brain and the body

Psychologists use various techniques and methods to understand how the brain is organised, how it functions and how it contributes to our behaviour. Some of these sound more glamorous than others – neuroimaging, for example, is seemingly more exciting than cataloguing the effects of brain injury. Both have an important function in psychology. Psychologists also use techniques that measure peripheral physical processes – blood pressure, heart rate, hormone and antibody secretion, electrodermal skin response, respiration, muscle contraction, and so on. By measuring the muscle activity of the face during various emotions, a technique called electromyography can detect changes in muscle activity that are invisible to the human eye but betray much about what a person is feeling. The electrodermal skin response is one of the elements of the polygraph, the so-called lie detector (invented by the man who also created Wonder Woman who, you might recall, used to foil ne'er do wells with her lasso of truth). The polygraph, though, is nothing of the kind – it detects changes in arousal, and lying tends to be associated with changes in arousal as indexed by changes in electrical potential on the skin (itself produced by sweating). Heart rate is measured by electrocardiography (ECG), and is an important variable in, for example, stress research (competitive people, who are at risk for cardiovascular disease, have a faster heart rate than co-operative people).

The most invasive technique that psychologists use is lesioning. In animals, this normally involves damaging a brain region of interest and examining the consequences. Neuropsychologists also study the effects of brain injury but that which occurs though head injury, surgery, disease, or illness (such as a stroke). Some people with brain injury develop highly unusual symptoms that might help explain (i) how the brain behaves when function is impaired; (ii) what this tells us about the way in which the brain behaves when normal; and (iii) how we undertake certain functions such as reading or speaking because the symptoms can be very specific. Some patients are unable to inhibit inappropriate thoughts and feelings; others fail to recognise objects or even their own and familiar others' faces; some appear to be 'blind' although the eyes and the visual system are intact, or suffer severe amnesia (memory loss). A condition called deep dyslexia is characterised by a severe impairment in the ability to read – words are misread as semantically similar ones (e.g. 'sleep' might be read as 'dream'). In another, called phonological dyslexia, patients are unable to read non-words or pseudo-words (e.g. splant). These conditions may tell us something about the way in which we learn to read (more on this in the language chapter).

Neuroimaging techniques either measure brain structure or function. Two techniques which measure structure are Computerised Tomography (CT) and Magnetic Resonance Imaging (MRI). CT, for example, exploits X-ray technology to produce a two-dimensional representation of brain structure (X-rays are passed through the head and the amount of radiation

passed through is measured). MRI involves placing the participant's head in a scanner while a magnetic field is passed over it.
Hydrogen molecules in the brain reverberate and the machine
scans and detects these reverberations. The activity is converted
into a scan. Both of these techniques have good spatial resolu-
tion – they provide a fairly detailed picture of brain structure.

Measures of activation include Positron Emission
Tomography (PET) and functional Magnetic Resonance
Imaging (fMRI). PET is invasive – it involves the injection of
radioactive glucose or water. The assumption behind this is that
brain cells that are metabolically active will attract more oxygen
or blood flow (blood delivers oxygen to energy-hungry cells).
The radiation accumulates in areas that are most active because
more blood goes there. The radioactive parts of the
glucose/water are called positrons. When these are emitted, the
scanner detects them, and regions of activation can be translated
into a coloured map of the brain. fMRI, on the other hand, is
non-invasive. Here, the oxygen consumption of cells is
measured. Note that these techniques do not measure neural
activity directly – only the processes important to cells such as
blood flow and oxygen consumption. fMRI is now more widely
used than PET, but both have been used to study brain activity
in healthy and unhealthy people – memory, perception, socia-
bility, personality, language, the senses, mental illness, violence,
and many other topics have been studied using these techniques.
One study, testing the hypothesis that we have different brain
regions responsible for processing inanimate and animate visual
stimuli, found that different brain areas were recruited during
the viewing of tools and the viewing of animals. Others have
reported a specific region in the brain that responds to faces, but
not other stimuli. Recently, fMRI has been used to study highly
complex behaviour such as how the brain helps us navigate
around a virtual version of London, respond to *The Simpsons* and
Seinfeld, and even how we respond to the face of a loved one.

The techniques have also been used to study how the brain reorganises itself after injury. For example, improvements in a patient's language after brain injury have been associated with greater activation in the right hemisphere as the patient undergoes rehabilitation. Language/speech is normally a left-hemisphere function and one theory of recovery holds that the right side takes over the function of the damaged left. Until neuroimaging, this theory could only be tested indirectly. Now, it can be observed directly.

Finally, a few of the other techniques used in psychology are: MEG (magnetoencephalography), which measures the magnetic fields generated by neurons (so, when a person is speaking, the region involved in speech should generate greater magnetic fields); EEG (electroencephalography), which measures brain electrical activity recorded from electrodes placed – usually – on the scalp (this has an essential role in detecting and monitoring illnesses such as epilepsy where the EEG trace is erratic; it can also be used to index the different stages of sleep; in fact, the stages of sleep are normally defined by EEG activity, as you'll see in the next chapter); and rTMS (repetitive Transcranial Magnetic Stimulation), which involves briefly stimulating parts of the brain by passing alternating magnetic fields over them using a special device that looks like a paddle. This can momentarily but harmlessly disrupt function and has been used to treat depression (not consistently well) and to study functions such as picture naming, verb generation, basic speech and so on.

Basic behaviours: hunger and sex

These behaviours appear here because they are probably our most basic, biological behaviours, i.e. low level (unlike understanding metaphors, driving in the rain, threading a needle, executing a symphony, or interpreting a facial expression in a loved one which says 'I think we should end our relationship'). They are sometimes called motivational behaviours because, simply, we are motivated (or driven) to do them. They satisfy an essential, often physiological, need. This satisfaction provides a degree of homeostasis – a state of stability or equilibrium in the body which allows us/it to perform at optimal level.

Hunger results from low levels of glucose, a simple sugar, and some fatty acids in the body (the stomach seems almost irrelevant to hunger; people with no stomach can still feel hungry). The body consumes more foods from which it derives glucose than it needs and so it stores the excess, which is converted into other materials, in muscle or fat. The period in which the body converts its intake into glucose to provide it with energy is called the absorptive phase. During the fasting phase, the body uses the energy derived from glucose to function. A key facilitator of this process is insulin, a hormone which allows glucose into cells. If insulin is not produced, the body cannot use its glucose, a condition called diabetes mellitus. When glucose drops, we are motivated to find food. If we cannot find any, the body will rely on its stores – usually, glycogen in muscles. Fats are usually the last to be converted back into glucose.

A fascinating phenomenon in the psychology of eating is sensory-specific satiety: the notion that our feelings of fullness, and ratings of a food's pleasantness, are determined by specific, sensory properties of the food that we eat, such as its colour, shape, taste and smell. For example, studies by Barbara and Edmund Rolls at Oxford University have shown that people eat more pasta when presented with three different shapes than one, more sweets of different colours than of one, and more of a four-course than a single-course meal (a plate of sausages, say). Our pleasantness rating of the ingested food decreases whereas the rating of uneaten food remains stable. For example, if you eat a plate of sausages to satiety, your judgement of the pleasantness of sausages will decline; if you are given another food to taste, however, you'll find it more pleasant and palatable.

There is a good reason for sensory-specific satiety: eating more than one type of food ensures that we ingest a variety of nutrients and, therefore, increases our potential for survival and good health. The part of the brain that seems to mediate satiety appears to be at the top end of the frontal lobe (a part called the orbitofrontal cortex): smelling food eaten to satiety (e.g. bananas) leads to a decrease in activation here; smelling foods not eaten (e.g. vanilla) results in activation. Similar results have been found with chocolate ingestion.

Sexual behaviour, unlike eating, is voluntary – there is no physiological need to have sex. Masters and Johnson's classic report of the 1960s showed that sex seems to progress through four stages: (i) excitement – self-explanatory, and occurring during initial contact, foreplay and intercourse; (ii) plateau – sustained sexual activity where excitement and arousal do not increase, but plateau; (iii) orgasm; and (iv) satiety. Men and women engage in sexual mental imagery and show vasocongestion – blood flow to the penis in men, the labia and the chest in women. Various brain regions are involved in thinking about and engaging in sexual behaviour, including the hypothalamus, the amygdala and the orbitofrontal cortex. A study from Stanford University in 2002 found that the right hemisphere was more active while men watched sexually explicit videos. There seems to be little overlap, however, in the areas of the brain activated in men and women during sexual arousal.

The role of neurotransmitters in sex is unclear – one, dopamine, seems to be increased during arousal whereas an increase in another (serotonin) decreases sexual arousal (antidepressants can lead to reduced sexual drive because of this). In terms of sexual orientation, heterosexual and homosexual men tend to have similar levels of the hormone testosterone, but there is some evidence suggesting differences between heterosexual and homosexual men in two parts of the hypothalamus.

Testosterone: the 'dominant' hormone

The hormone testosterone has an important role in psychology because it has very curious effects on behaviour. For example, high levels have been associated with social status, rank and dominance. The evidence linking high levels of testosterone specifically with aggressive behaviour is mixed although some studies report correlations between testosterone in violent offenders and the degree of violence shown in their crime, and find that women offenders who produce unprovoked violence have higher levels than women who do not. Men who see their team lose at football show a drop in testosterone. A study of five men left alone to survive on a boat found that the levels of testosterone shifted as dominance patterns were formed: the more dominant the man, the greater the testosterone.

Testosterone tends to be low in married men. A recent study also found that it was higher in single men than those in a long-distance relationship or those living with a partner. (The same pattern was found in women.) Another study found that women who regarded themselves as dominant had higher levels of testosterone. Dominance is highly correlated with testosterone. Men with low testosterone look around a room tentatively when entering whereas men with high testosterone enter more directly. A recent experiment examined how individuals with either low or high testosterone would cope when put in a very dominant, or non-dominant, position. When low testosterone men were placed in the dominant position, they were more emotionally aroused, focused more on their status and performed badly. High testosterone individuals showed the same pattern but only when placed in a less dominant position. There is also evidence that testosterone affects empathy. A study in which people were administered the hormone and asked to empathise with a series of emotional facial expressions found that these participants mimicked the faces less than those who did not receive testosterone.

Drugs and behaviour: psychopharmacology

Other substances have a more direct and dramatic effect on behaviour. Drugs administered by doctors relieve distress or pain, but they can have behavioural consequences such as heightened awareness or euphoria. Drugs act on brain receptors and can be administered orally, rectally, by decongestant, by inhalation, by injection (the fastest method), or via the skin (by patches). Brain receptors are specialised and respond to certain drugs and various factors affect how we respond to them – from strength of dose, to previous experience, to metabolism, to whether they have been combined with other drugs such as alcohol. Some of the drugs that have the most profound effect on our behaviour and consciousness either sedate or stimulate.

Sedatives are CNS depressants and relieve anxiety or produce sedation/sleepiness. Physical activity is reduced, we feel drowsy and our cognitive abilities deteriorate. The most common of these is alcohol (ethyl alcohol or ethanol) which is rapidly absorbed into the blood stream (it takes between thirty and ninety minutes from the time of the last drink for blood to reach its maximum alcohol concentration). Drunkenness is achieved when alcohol concentration in the blood is 0.08%, although the figure is arbitrary and different countries have different levels at which driving is dangerous (usually between 0.05 and 0.08%, when accidents are four times as likely).

Psychostimulants stimulate the activity of neurotransmitters. These have little medical value but they produce dramatic psychological effects. Cocaine is one example. Between twenty and thirty million people in the USA are thought to be cocaine users – usually between twelve and thirty-nine years old, male, and alcohol dependent. It is derived from the Peruvian and Bolivian coca tree whose leaves contain the alkaloid. Coca-Cola once included cocaine and was marketed proudly as having it. In powdered form, cocaine is sold as cocaine hydrochloride ('crystal', 'snow'); when boiled dry it is called crack (after the noise it makes when boiled). Symptoms of cocaine use include alertness, hyperactivity, pupil dilation, talkativeness, extreme euphoria (these last about thirty minutes, leading to a milder sixty to ninety minute period, then hours of anxiety).

Caffeine's effects are less pronounced, mercifully. An average cup of coffee contains 50–150mg of caffeine; a small bottle of cola around 35–55mg. A lethal dose is 10g (or 100 cups of coffee). Ingesting 2–5g stimulates the spinal cord and this is not a good thing. It's absorbed very quickly and has a half-life of three and a half to five hours (the period is shorter in smokers; longer in children). Caffeine increases heart rate, constricts blood vessels, and stimulates the cortex. It makes us alert and wakeful, but also restless and affects our psychomotor performance (try completing one of those games at a fair where you have to direct a hoop along an undulating electric coil without touching it, after a couple of cups of strong coffee). Anxiety, insomnia, and mood change are side effects.

Nicotine is one of about 4000 compounds released by tobacco (and is not carcinogenic) and between 0.5 to 2mg of it is found in a typical cigarette. Once absorbed, nicotine quickly acts on the brain. It stimulates the brainstem (which might explain why people feel like vomiting when they try their first cigarette – this structure is responsible for this act). It reduces muscle tone and weight gain, and increases blood pressure and heart rate. It acts on various receptors, especially ones called acetylcholine receptors.

Marijuana/cannabis is a mild sedative derived from the hemp plant, *Cannabis sativa*. The active ingredient (the one it is smoked for) is delta-9-tetrahydrocannabinol (THC). A typical joint will contain between 150 and 300mg of THC and the ingredient can remain in the body for up to thirty days. The US National Survey on Drug Use and Health in 2006 estimated that 97.8 million North Americans had used cannabis at least once (approximately forty per cent of the population). When asked if they had used cannabis in the past month, 16.3% of 18–25 year olds and 4.2% of the over-26s reported using it. US prisoner use of cannabis is even higher – approximately seventy-seven per cent of State prisoners indicated that they had used it.

Cannabis use is usually associated with relaxation, reduced anxiety, hallucinations, intense emotional experiences (at high doses), heightened sensation and warped time perception. Reaction time and co-ordination are impaired: it has been estimated that the second most commonly found substance in drivers involved in accidents or fatalities is cannabis. There is also evidence that patients treated for cannabis-induced psychotic symptoms have a forty to fifty per cent chance of developing the symptoms of schizophrenia. Other studies, however, suggest that it can alleviate pain and provide relief from nausea in multiple sclerosis and chemotherapy.

Opioids do have a medical purpose – they are substances absorbed by the body which produce analgesia or pain relief. The most well-known is opium, derived from the opium poppy, *Papaver somniferum*. Substances derived from the poppy are called opiates and the most common are morphine and codeine (the second acts on the brainstem which regulates coughing, hence the use of codeine as a cough suppressant). Opioids act on three types of brain receptors and morphine, the most effective analgesic, acts on the mu type receptor, producing euphoria, slowness of breathing, constipation, and miosis (pin-point pupils). Methadone, a synthetic opioid, has the same effect as morphine and is used to wean heroin-addicts off heroin. Diacetyl morphine (heroin) is three times more powerful than morphine and reaches the brain more quickly.

The evolution of behaviour

A discussion of the biology of behaviour is not complete without reference to Darwin. Darwin's theory of evolution had a dramatic effect on the course of science and psychology's role in it. According to the theory, species either adapt effectively or ineffectively to changes in our environment (this is called adaptation). Variations in species will be passed on to the next generation, through natural selection, itself achieved through reproduction. This variation together with the ability to adapt (in competition with others who also need the resources we do) ensures the evolution of the species.

In recent years, some psychologists have proposed that evolutionary mechanisms could explain behaviour such as altruism, physical attraction, the desire to remain monogamous, or to aggress towards kin who are not blood relatives (this new field is called evolutionary psychology or EP). EP is essentially an extension of another theory related to evolution: sociobiology, proposed by E.O. Wilson in his book, *Sociobiology: The New Synthesis*, published in 1975. Sociobiology is the study of the biological basis of social behaviour. A tenet of sociobiology, proposed by the geneticist William Hamilton in the 1960s, is inclusive fitness. That is, natural selection favours the reproductive success of those who share the same genes. This explains why family members are more likely to be altruistic to other family members than to strangers: the closer the relationship, the more likely (and pronounced) the altruism. This helps protect and, by extension, prolong the gene pool. That said, psychological research has indicated that this relationship is not consistent and is mediated by how *emotionally* close you feel to a relative. The most famous evidence for inclusive fitness is data on assault in stepfamilies: physical harm and assault is more common in stepfamilies and murders are more common in cohabiting couples than married ones (with men doing the murdering).

If altruism is designed to extend our gene pool, why, then, do we commit altruistic acts with non-family members? Simply, because we work more effectively as a species if we co-operate with each other. It's telling that the characteristics we most admire in a partner – kindness, dependability, emotional stability and intelligence – are close to altruism.

Sociobiologists see humans as 'fitness maximisers' but evolutionary psychologists disagree. One of EP's most famous advocates, Donald Buss, asks that if we are all fitness maximisers, why are men not cueing up at sperm banks, itching to donate their emissions? Why do we prefer fatty foods (which are detrimental to us in the long run)?

Evolutionary psychologists see humans as being 'adaptation executors' – we evolve mechanisms for dealing with certain tasks (whether seeking food or a mate) and these differ depending on the task. It is known that men (especially those in the West), prefer a female body with a low waist to hip ratio (WHR) – more fat is deposited on the buttocks and hips. This size is thought to reflect women's reproductive health and potential. In certain cultures (where there is no exposure to our media and its obsession, right or wrong, with physical appearance), such as the Matsigenka culture of Peru, men prefer a higher WHR, i.e. positively plump ladies. Western groups, when asked to rate WHR for healthiness, find low WHR to be healthier; non-westernised samples prefer a high WHR. Western men also prefer women with a lower Body Mass Index (a score that reflects weight, taking into account height). So as not to leave men out of this shallow-fest, women also have a shape preference. They prefer a man with a triangular-shaped upper body (a low waist to chest ratio).

Men and women seek different characteristics in a partner and these are thought to be evolutionary in origin. Heterosexual men prefer women who are physically attractive, whereas women place greater emphasis on non-physical features such as resources. The evolutionary explanation for this is that women who fall pregnant have to discharge responsibility and care for the foetus for a period of many months: choosing a partner who will be reliable, dependable and share in parenting is, therefore, essential. Men, on the other hand, have no immediate, physical responsibility to discharge; they can, therefore, seek many partners.

Infidelity is international and it's been estimated that between twenty and fifty per cent of married couples will be unfaithful to their partner at some point. (One study found that eighty-four per cent of undergraduates reported being the target of 'mate-poaching'.) Men are more likely to be jealous if their partner has been sexually unfaithful; women if their partner has been emotionally unfaithful (having a deep, non-sexual, loving relationship with another woman). The more disagreeable, emotionally unstable and undependable a partner is, the more likely it is that he or she will be cuckolded. Mate-poachers tend to be less agreeable or conscientious, have strong sexual desires and are also sexually attractive. Getting a partner drunk works as a short-term strategy, but it is not effective in the long term.

Women, however, do not always go for the most good-looking, successful man. A recent study found that when women were given identical lonely hearts ads where the man's occupation varied, and these were paired with photographs of attractive, average or unattractive men, the women preferred the attractive man of moderate socio-economic status, over the attractive man who was a high-flyer. One explanation is that snapping up the latter would lead to fending off too much competition – all the ladies would be after this type and so he would be more likely to be unfaithful because of the many blandishments and opportunities that would come his way.

Understanding the biological bases of behaviour is important to psychology – the activity of the CNS is what gives rise to almost all of our basic and complex behaviour. In the next chapter, you will see how psychology has studied two of the seemingly basic but actually very complex behaviours – sensation and perception – and the chapter also gives an overview of three elements of consciousness: attention, sleep, and hypnosis.

3

Sensing and perceiving the world

How can we tell a Mozart symphony from a 50 cent cacophony, a butterfly in flight from an overhead plane, a lover's face from a stranger's, a painful punch from a caress, the whiff of a greasy hamburger from the scent of a seared scallop?

Our sensory systems are some of the most complex in the body and each allows us to experience the world in its rich, frequently drab, occasionally challenging form. Psychologists distinguish between two phenomena: sensation and perception. Sensation involves the detection of single elements of a stimulus we experience – such as its colour, brightness, loudness, and so on. Perception involves the detection of stimuli, by movement, location, background, and so on. So, detecting the colour yellow is a sensation; detecting a banana is a perception. Seeing a moving object is a sensation; identifying the object as a car is a perception.

We are used to hearing that we have five senses: vision (seeing), audition (hearing), gustation (tasting), olfaction (smelling), and somatosensation (touching/being touched). But, in reality, there are many more. Take somatosensation – this can involve the detection of warmth, coolness, physical harm, vibration, leg and arm movement, muscular contraction, and others. These are, in a sense, different senses.

Information received by the senses is detected by specialised sensory organs and sent to specific areas of the brain. The process whereby our sense organs convert energy from this information into neural activity is called transduction. When we detect this information, the brain needs to make sense of it, to code it in some way. One way is via anatomical coding. If you rub your eyes, you stimulate light-sensitive receptors that, via the optic nerve, send action potentials to the brain. The brain has no way of knowing that this stimulation has been produced by something artificial (your rubbing) and so responds as if it has just been stimulated by light. Hence, you see stars or flashes of light. Patients during surgery who have specific areas of the brain electrically stimulated can report taste or sound sensations, even though they have not actually tasted or heard anything. This coding is specific to senses and to stimuli within each sense – we can tell the difference between a brush of the cheek and a tap on the knee, for example, because different nerve fibres respond to stimulation of different parts of the body.

The body can also detect intensity, and engages in temporal coding – a light touch produces a low rate of firing; a forceful one, a high rate. The study of the detection of such differences is called psychophysics and, in the nineteenth century, the anatomist Ernst Weber suggested a measurement called the just noticeable difference – the smallest change in the magnitude of sensation that is detectable (such as telling whether one object is heavier than another). Of course, this gets complicated, if more interesting, when senses interact. One study found that when workers complained that the black boxes they had to shift in one American factory were very heavy, and the supervisor changed the colour of the boxes to a lighter colour over the weekend, the workers returned on Monday and said that the boxes felt a lot lighter. The actual weight had not changed. There are also people who claim that stimuli in one modality (say, taste) generate sensations in another (such as touch). The composer Liszt, for example, claimed to see colours when hearing specific notes. This phenomenon is called synaesthesia and seems to be reliable in those who report it (and is probably attributable to special, dysfunctional, connections between the two brain areas representing these senses).

Seeing

Vision is our most dominant sense – if you ask people which sense they would least like to live without, it would be vision (not surprisingly, smell is the one people think they could do without). Our eyes are very sensitive to light, which has a specific wavelength, and visible light with different wavelengths give off a different colour (red or blue, for example). The part of the light wavelength we can detect is called the visible spectrum (part of the electromagnetic spectrum). We can't detect ultraviolet radiation but bees can (and some flowers exhibit certain light wavelengths to produce this, thus attracting them).

The eye, although it may not seem so, is a well-protected delicate organ: eyebrows, lids, lashes, skull sockets and the reflex to shut when seeing a fast approaching object, all help protect it. The eye has various parts that serve important functions. The transparent cornea (the only transparent bit of the body) is the bulge at the front of the eye covered by a tough membrane, the sclera. The iris controls the amount of light let in and is controlled by two muscles which alter the size of the pupil, making it constrict when there is much light, and dilate when there is little.

The fluid behind the cornea, the aqueous fluid, keeps the cornea functioning (if there is too much, it causes a condition called glaucoma). The lens, found behind the iris, allows images to be focused on the back surface of the eye. The image is upside down, and left and right are reversed, although we 'see' the image properly. The iris can also change shape to allow it to see nearby and distant objects (a process called accommodation). If the eyeball is too long, people will be near-sighted; if it is too short, people will be far-sighted.

The surface at the back of the eye is the retina and this contains over 130 million neurons (called photoreceptors) that transduce light into neural activity. The back of the eye also features the optic disk – because there are no photoreceptors in front of it, this gives us a blind spot. You can demonstrate this for yourself by looking at figure 4. Close your left eye and look at the cross with your right eye. Move the book back and forth, towards you and away from you. At around a distance of 20cm, the 'Y' should disappear because the image falls on your blind spot.

The retina has two types of photoreceptors: rods and cones (about 125 million of the first, six million of the second), so-called because of their shape. Rods respond to dim light, cones to brightness. Both are involved in colour vision. A small part at the back of the retina, the fovea, contains only cones and allows detailed vision.

Transduction in vision is complex but, in essence, photoreceptors contain four kinds of photopigment (made up of two molecules: vitamin A and protein) which, when light reaches them, split into the two molecules. This causes a chemical chain reaction (there are three element pairs in the chain) that

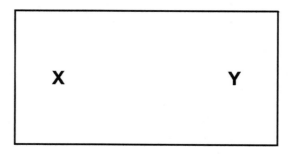

Figure 4 Demonstration of the blind spot

ultimately leads to a signal being sent to the brain. The photopigment of rods, rhodopsin, is pink, and it is this which is responsible for our being unable to adjust quickly to the light indoors after we have been in bright sunlight (when light splits a photopigment, the photopigment loses its colour). It eventually allows us to sense the indoor light normally because the photoreceptor has caused the two molecules to re-combine (a process called dark adaptation).

How can we tell yellow from red? The eye contains three types of cone, each of which contains a different photopigment which is sensitive to light of a particular wavelength (i.e. light that makes molecules split): it is these which allow us to detect different colours. A wavelength of 540 nanometres, for example, is sensed as green.

A feature of the visual system, however, is that it is synthetic – it brings things together – rather than analytic (takes them apart, like the auditory system). When two or more lights of different wavelengths are combined, therefore, we get colour mixing. This is not like mixing paint – that simply subtracts colour; mixing blue and yellow paint gives you green (darker than yellow), but mixing two wavelengths always gives a brighter colour (shining red and green wavelengths on a white background, for example, produces yellow). One well-known theory of colour, the trichromatic theory, developed by British polymath Thomas Young in 1802, argued that the eye had three types of colour receptor and the brain synthesised information from all three. The receptors were sensitive to blue, green and red. The theory has since been incorporated into more elaborate ones. We know that cones contain three types of photopigment that absorb specific wavelengths of light: blue-violet, green, and yellow-green (there are fewer blue ones) and that there are two types of specialised cells (ganglion cells) that encode colour vision (red/green cells and yellow/blue cells). These cells are also responsible for producing after images.

Some people can't detect colour normally and most of these are men because the gene for producing photopigment is located on one of men's chromosomes. Some have a photopigment missing and use two primary colours for matching (they are called dichromats); some have altered photopigments (anomalous trichromats). Around one per cent of men lack the photopigment for 'red' cones and so reds and oranges are seen as very dark colours (a disorder called protanopia); some have 'green' cones filled with 'red' photopigment (deuteranopia). Finally, some people see the world in green and red – a blue sky, therefore, looks bright green (tritanopia), but this is a rare condition and involves the blue cones.

On the subject of seeing red, a study published in *Nature* found that Olympians from the 2004 games who dressed in red for boxing, tae kwondo, freestyle wrestling, and Greco-Roman wrestling won more often than did those dressed in blue; the same was found for winners in Euro 2004. Another study, published in a 2007 issue of the *Journal of Experimental Psychology: General*, found that (even brief) exposure to the colour red impaired cognitive performance. One theory to explain this suggests that red is associated with dominance and aggression and is avoided by most people, hence the combat sport success and the inferior thinking in its presence.

Perception

When we see, we don't usually perceive individual features of an object (percepts); we perceive things as cars, trees, people, and so on. We notice where they are, whether they are moving. An important part of identifying an object's form is its boundary but we can sometimes see more than one object in one stimulus.

We also group objects to make sense of what we see – we create a gestalt (from the German for 'form'). In figure 5, for example, we see two imaginary triangles ('illusory contours'). This example illustrates the principle of closure: we provide the missing information to make a complete object. Another principle is called good continuation. In figure 6, for example, it is easier for us to imagine the line being continuous rather than branching off.

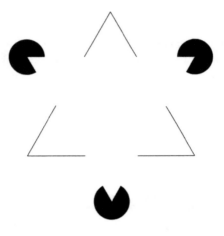

Figure 5 In this image, we tend to see a triangle because of the notched stimuli

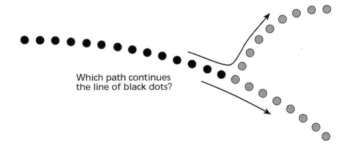

Figure 6 We tend to prefer to see stimuli as continuous, rather than tangential

One view of why we recognise objects is that, through experience, we develop a template of what objects look like. Another argues that we are better at detecting familiar objects if these have distinctive features. Try the following exercise. Find the letter Z in the two columns in figure 7.

You probably found the letter more quickly in the left-hand column. This experiment was reported by Neisser in 1964. In the left-hand column, the Z shares few features with the other letters and is, therefore, more distinctive; in the right-hand column, it shares many features. The same phenomenon arises when you search for the letter A amongst Bs – this is easier than finding a B amongst As – or finding orange-coloured objects amongst red ones, or a tilted object amongst vertical ones.

GDOROC	IVEMXW
COQUCD	XVIWME
DUCOQG	VEMIXW
GRUDQO	WEKMVI
OCDURQ	XIMVWE
DUCGRO	IVMWEX
ODUCQG	VWEMXI
CQOGRD	IMEWXV
DUZORQ	EXMZWI
UCGROD	IEMWVX
QCUDOG	EIVXWM
RQGUDO	WXEMIV
DRGOQC	MIWVXE
OQGDRU	IMEVXW
UGCODQ	IEMWVX
ODRUCQ	IMWVEX
UDQRGC	XWMVEI
ORGCUD	IWEVXM

Figure 7 Certain letters are found more quickly when embedded in some letters than others

The psychologist Biederman developed this idea further by arguing that we recognise objects based on an understanding of thirty-six different types of shape (called geons). There is some evidence for this – we can recognise incomplete drawings of objects, for example, if we see particular features such as cusps and joints. While this sounds a smart idea when perceiving a book or a cup, it is less persuasive in helping us understand how we recognise complex stimuli such as a familiar face. It is unlikely that we identify a best friend by putting together a collection of geons.

Context is also important to visual perception. Take a look at the geons in figure 8. Can you tell what they represent?

Now, take a look at them in context (in figure 9) and they make sense. This is an example of top-down processing: the

Figure 8 Assorted geons

Figure 9 Geons as part of an object

Figure 10 Examples of top-down and bottom-up processing. We can identify the words – or, at least, assume they are certain words – despite the obscuring (or unusual letter forms)

overall context allows us to process the information we perceive. The opposite, bottom-up processing, is where we use individual features to process information about what we see. Sometimes, though, we use both, as in the example in figure 10.

Perhaps one of the most important social and personal acts of visual perception we engage in is face perception and we are good at it – we can determine the sex, age and colour of a face quickly. Men have larger noses, more prominent brows, more deeply set eyes. Women have fuller cheeks, less facial hair, smaller noses, larger eyes and a shorter upper lip. The best facial clue to a person's sex is the eyes, followed by the nose. A three-quarter profile is better for recognition than is a full-frontal photograph.

The attractiveness of a face is unrelated to how distinctive it is. In the nineteenth century, Francis Galton proposed that the more average-looking the face, the more attractive it would be. Experiments by David Perrett, from St Andrews University, and others, however, using special morphing computer technology which manipulates the attractiveness of male and female faces to create composite photographs (of very attractive, attractive, and average faces), have found that the 'attractive' composite is rated as much more desirable than is the 'average' composite. The more attractive faces had higher cheek bones, thinner jaws, larger eyes relative to the size of the face, and a shorter distance between mouth and chin.

Faces are also interesting in that they tend to be asymmetrical – the left and right sides are subtly different. Take a digital photo of your face and, using image manipulation software, split this down the middle and create a mirror image for each side. You'll see a difference. Some evolutionary psychologists have linked more symmetrical faces to better health and more successful mating strategy – the more symmetrical the face, the more attractive and healthy it is rated (there are some physiological reasons why this should be). Dancers with more symmetrical bodies are also rated as more attractive (and as better dancers). Whether we prefer masculine faces or feminine ones is unclear – there is some evidence that women prefer more masculine faces, and more dominant men, during the fertile phase of their cycle (reflecting a need for a strong, assertive partner) and when their testosterone level is highest.

There is evidence that one region of the brain – the fusiform gyrus or human face area – is specialised for face recognition. Neuroimaging evidence shows that this area is more active when people see faces than other stimuli. A nearby brain area may be specialised for recognising a different class of stimuli, landmarks. Damage to other parts of the brain produces some unusual perceptual disorders. People with visual agnosia, for example, are unable to recognise simple objects, despite being able to make good drawings of them. One famous case study, HJA, was able to render a tremendously detailed drawing of a building but was unable to name the object. People with blindsight have damage to the primary visual cortex and are blind in a part of their visual field – they will claim not to be able to see something if an object is presented, even thought their visual system is intact. However, if it is moved, the patient will indicate that they perceived something. Others have an extraordinary condition called prosopagnosia – where damage to the back of the brain renders people unable to recognise familiar faces (although they can identify the sex, race and so on, in a face). One case study described a very irritable diner who became annoyed because a fellow restaurant patron was staring at him throughout his meal. Having had enough of this, the diner called over the waiter and complained. The waiter listened. And then politely told the man that he had been staring at his own reflection.

Finally, patients with damage to the back of the right side of the brain may be unable to attend to one half of the world, or visual field (usually, the left). If asked to draw a clock, for example, they will either crowd the numbers one to twelve on the right or will only include the numbers one to six. The Italian film director Federico Fellini suffered from this condition – spatial hemineglect – following a stroke. Being an accomplished cartoonist, he'd doodle on the right side of the tests he was given, neglecting the left side.

As psychological egoists, we believe that what we perceive must be what others perceive. Is this right? Experience of the viewed objects is clearly important. The psychologist Jan Deregowski found that when the Me'en tribe of Ethiopia were shown pictures from a children's colouring book, they would sniff them, listen to the pages, examine the paper texture ... but ignore the pictures. The culture was unfamiliar with photographs – they only paid attention to pictures of the indigenous animals.

People who live in 'carpentered' cultures where buildings are made of strong, straight materials which meet at right angles are more susceptible than 'uncarpentered' cultures to the famous Muller-Lyer illusion. You can see this illustrated in figure 11. Which vertical line in these two images is the longest?

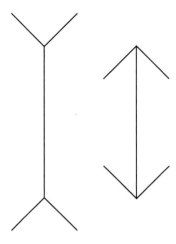

Figure 11 The Muller-Lyer illusion

Most people in Western, carpentered cultures would say the line on the left although they are both actually the same length.

Recent research has also shown that 'Western' people tend to perceive objects in a more analytical, focused way whereas East Asians are more likely to attend to the context in which objects appear (i.e. they perceive a scene 'holistically'). In one study where American and Japanese participants were asked to describe an underwater scene, Americans were more likely to describe objects in the water but the Japanese reported sixty per cent more information about the background environment.

In a different scenario, Americans identified an object (a tiger) more accurately than did the Japanese when it appeared against a different background to that in which it was originally seen. One reason for this might be the types of eye movement made by different cultures. Americans, for example, tend to focus on specific objects and focus more quickly on them whereas the Chinese make more saccades – eye movements – to the background.

Colour perception and naming has been widely studied cross-culturally. William Gladstone noted in the mid-nineteenth century that ancient Greek writing did not include words for 'brown' or 'blue'. One view held that the language we use influences our perception of the environment, and, in fact, our thought (this is the linguistic relativity hypothesis, later known as the Sapir-Whorf hypothesis). The relevance of this to colour is that different cultures would give different names to what they perceived, thus describing many different shades and hues (like the famed, if probably apocryphal, fact that Eskimos have tens of words for 'snow'). Two anthropologists, Berlin and Kay, discovered that eleven primary colour terms were found in the cultures they studied; some, such as the Dani culture of New Guinea, used only two (black and white); Russian had two words for blue. Where languages had names for primary colours, they tended to be black, red and white. Across cultures, primary colours tended to be more familiar and, therefore, better recognised. When asked to remember names for colour chips, for example, even the dual-word Dani learned words faster if they were associated with primary colours.

Does extra-sensory perception exist?

No.

Hearing

According to a survey by an acoustic engineering professor at Salford University, the three worst sounds in the world are vomiting, microphone feedback and wailing babies (see www.sound101.org). When an object vibrates, it causes the air around it to move. As this air reaches your ear, your eardrum is bent; as it moves away, it is pushed out. This is sound (or a soundwave, measured in hertz). We can detect differences in vibration ranging from 30 to 20,000Hz.

The outer part of our ear (the pinna, which we often call the ear but is only the external part of it) helps funnel sound towards the apparatus that does the hard auditory work: first, the eardrum, a membrane which vibrates in and out when sound waves reach it, followed by the ossicles (three small bones) which transmit the vibrations of the eardrum to the inner ear, which is filled with fluid and contains the receptor organ for sound, itself contained in a bony structure called the cochlea. The cochlea is divided into two by the basilar membrane, a sheet of tissue that contains the auditory receptor cells, and which varies in width and flexibility so that different frequencies of sound cause different parts to vibrate.

Sound has three essential perceptual qualities: loudness, pitch and timbre. It is the last which allows us to discriminate between the variety of sounds to which we are exposed because it combines pitch with the perception of an object's overtones. It is timbre that allows us to tell the different instruments in an orchestra apart.

Neuroimaging research suggests that different parts of the brain are responsible for sensing different types of sound such as tones, non-speech sound, speech and meaningless speech, and that different parts are involved in the production and perception of sound and our emotional response to it (some patients with damage to a specific part of the temporal lobe, for example, find discordant music more pleasant than uninjured people do). There are different parts of the auditory cortex that respond to hearing one's own name and that of another. In one study, participants heard the first five notes to the US soap-opera *Dallas*, and were asked to imagine the rest, as blood flow in their brain was measured. The right auditory (association) cortex and part of the motor area were activated when they imagined the rest of the tune (although it is also possible that such activation was due to people thinking about implausible plot lines and slightly unconventional acting; number seven in the top ten worst noises was argument in a soap opera).

Sight and sound can interact in interesting ways: imagine a burly, six-foot-four football player talking after inhaling helium. The oxymoron is amusing, but other interactions are more psychologically meaningful. For example, in an experiment where one flash of light was accompanied by several auditory beeps, people reported seeing multiple flashes (not one). When the space between each beep was lengthened, the illusion became weaker. In another study, people looked at two visual stimuli passing through each other while a sound was made at the point of passing. When a sound was heard, participants thought that the two images had collided; when there was no sound, the stimuli were described as streaming through each other. It is as if participants were filling in the blanks: we expect two objects that 'collide' to make a noise; the brain was simply computing what it was expecting to compute.

Smell and taste

The two most important senses for allowing us to appreciate food are smell and taste, but one is more important than the other (and it probably isn't the one you think). Approximately eighty per cent of food flavour comes from olfaction – smell receptors at the back of the throat and the top of the nose are what allow us to identify food through the release of olfactory molecules. We can discriminate between thousands of different odours but there are only five basic tastes – sour, sweet, bitter, salty and umami (a savoury taste characteristic of monosodium glutamate). It has also been suggested that 'metallic' should be added to this list. Incidentally, the oft-paraded diagrams in textbooks labelling certain parts of the tongue as localised for certain tastes are a myth – each region of the tongue can experience more than one different 'taste'.

The limited sensory range of taste means that food only imparts these sensations to the taste buds. When we have a cold, we can usually detect food's taste, but not identify the food (we say we can't taste anything, but we can). This is due to an impairment in the functioning of the olfactory receptors. 'When smell is intercepted,' wrote Jean-Anthelme Brillat-Savarin in *The Physiology of Taste* in 1825, 'taste is paralysed'. Substitute flavour for taste and that's quite a good summary.

Smell and taste are described as chemical senses because they detect molecules in the environment. Smell is unusual because it is the only sense whose receptors are directly exposed to the environment (located at the top of the inside of the nose). It has also been called the Cinderella of the senses because it is the least-loved and most dispensable sense. Its role in life, however, is more important than we think – we need it to appreciate food, to warn us of danger (smoke, gas, spoiled food) and to make life pleasurable (perfume, the scent of a lover). There was some suggestion made some decades ago that humans produce pheromones – chemicals that elicit stereotypical responses, usually sexual ones. For example, in sows, the pheromone, androstenone, makes them adopt the mating position – vets can buy this in an aerosol can, called *Boarmate* (sows are used to detect truffles because the fungus contains this steroid). There is little evidence, however, that androstenone makes humans more sexually attractive to the opposite sex. In fact, perfume works much better (although see below) – in one study, the scent of a man's cologne increased women's sexual arousal if the women were engaged in sexual fantasy during the late, follicular, stage of their menstrual cycle.

The presence of pleasant odour can increase (and decrease) vigilance, improve clerical work, enhance helping, benefit encoding and recall of events (the so-called Proust effect, after the French novelist whose autobiographical mammoth work, *A la Recherché du Temps Perdu*, was prompted by the scent of a madeleine cake dipped in tea), enhance pain perception (there is no evidence that smelling a pleasant odour has any medium- to long-term beneficial effect on health), alter brain activation, and improve aspects of driving performance. Perfume, however, can be a hindrance. An American study from the 1980s showed that formally dressed women interviewees who wore perfume were liked less, and rated as more cold and manipulative by their potential employers. Informally dressed women wearing perfume were less negatively judged. (However, the perfume was called 'Jungle Gardenia'.)

The receptors for taste are on the tongue and three cranial nerves transmit information from here to the thalamus, described in chapter 2, and then on to the cortex. There appear to be two regions in the brain that allow us to process taste – one allows us to detect the sensory properties of food; the other responds to the hedonic quality of food (its pleasantness). For example, food eaten to satiety and which becomes unpleasant leads to a reduction in the latter but not the former.

Our sense of taste is malleable, as is our sense of smell. If a newborn is given sweetened water at six months, it will prefer sweetened water when tested a year later. The same phenomenon occurs with salt. We are notoriously poor at identifying or naming odours and can often be conned into thinking we are smelling something we are not. One cross-cultural study found that forty per cent of Germans sniffing Vicks vapour rub thought it represented an edible substance; twenty-five per cent of a Japanese sample thought the same about India ink.

Somatosensation

Our body senses, somatosenses, allow us to experience temperature, pressure, and pain (the sensation of pain is called nociception). Our most sensitive body parts are the lips and fingertips. Noxious stimuli can elicit at least two types of pain: sharp or 'bright' pain, followed by dull, throbbing pain. As much as we dislike it, we need to experience pain because it is the best motivator for surviving: it is the body's way of telling us that we are damaged (and that we may not survive if the pain is prolonged and the damage is not treated).

Paying attention

Research suggests that pain can be reduced if we are distracted and almost everything we've read about so far requires attention and consciousness. Consciousness itself does not exist: it is a name that we give to an organism's state and, if we're honest, science gave the term and its study a very wide berth until the 1990s when there was an explosion of interest in studying the topic, exemplified by books such as Daniel Dennett's *Consciousness Explained* and Francis Crick's *Astonishing Hypothesis*. Attention, however, has been part of the psychologist's stock-in-trade for decades.

Clearly, when we perceive, there are some things we have to ignore (there are some things the brain will not allow us to pay attention to — it simply can't cope with that amount of information). When reading, we read a word or phrase at a time, not whole pages (although some people with eidetic — or photographic — memory can memorise pages of text). We are aware of the surrounding words, the white of the page, the outline of the cover, even objects in the background, behind the book, but we tend not to pay specific attention to them (unless we are bored). Similarly, when we're in conversation with someone at a party, we focus on the person we are speaking to, not on every conversation in the room. That would be impossible. In these examples, and many others, we are engaging in selective attention. Sometimes we are forced to attend – such as when we hear a loud noise; sometimes we are instructed to – when we listen to safety instructions on a plane or boat; sometimes we attend because of task demands – driving a car, for example. The first demonstration of selective attention in the laboratory was done using dichotic listening – this is where sentences are presented to each ear via headphones and people are asked to repeat one of the sentences out loud. Even when the voice in the other, unattended ear was speaking in a foreign language, the selective attention was so successful, participants didn't notice.

Let's go back to the party scene above. Imagine you are deep in conversation but, although you are hanging onto every word you are listening to, you suddenly hear your own name being mentioned in another part of the room. This is an example of the cocktail-party effect, first reported in the 1950s. People who are capable of blocking irrelevant information generally are less likely to show this effect.

Noise and distraction

Unwanted noise tends to impair attention, as does distraction. The music we play may enhance our attention to a task at hand, but the loud, monotonous, vibrating Franz Ferdinand coming from the flat next door might drive us up the wall. Children who live next to busy airports report sleeping less and also perform less well on cognitive tasks. Of course, the most visible exemplar of a distractor nowadays is the mobile phone and many countries have banned the use of drivers' hand-held sets. The banning, however, seems misguided because psychological research shows that it is not only holding a phone that distracts a driver but the conversation he or she is having. This impairs driving performance more than does listening to the radio, demonstrating that it is not simply noise that disrupts driving but cognitively interacting with another person.

The psychology of consciousness: sleep

Sleep is usually regarded as a state of unconsciousness but is actually a state of altered consciousness. We go through various stages of sleep, characterised by specific psychophysiological features (measured by EEG and EMG, described earlier). These are:

Stage 1 – transition from wakefulness to sleep; muscles are still active, eyes roll around

Stage 2 – sleep deepens

Stage 3 – slow-wave sleep (so-called because of the type of EEG seen); environmental stimuli that would have woken us up in stage 1 have little effect here

Stage 4 – slow-wave sleep; reached within thirty minutes; respiration becomes irregular, as does heart rate; EEG looks like that seen during stage 1, paradoxically; muscles are relaxed but hands and feet might twitch; a person might sleep walk or talk; a child might exhibit a sleep disorder called enuresis (bed-wetting)

In stage 4, the eyes dart rapidly back and forth and up and down – the person is dreaming and is showing REM (rapid eye movement) sleep. This lasts between twenty and thirty minutes and is followed by an hour of slow-wave sleep. In this sense, sleep follows a ninety-minute cycle – REM sleep, followed by slow-wave sleep. This ninety-minute cycle also applies to many other behaviours – eating, drinking, smoking, urine production, and others – and has been called the Basic Rest Activity Cycle.

When people are deprived of sleep, the outcome is not pretty. In 2001, Gary Hart, a thirty-seven-year-old builder from Lincolnshire, UK, drove his Land Rover off the M62 motorway into the pathway of an oncoming east coast train. Ten men were killed, seventy-six people were injured. He admitted having had only a short nap in the past twenty-four hours.

A large body of research, much of it pioneered by Jim Horne at Loughborough University, UK, has demonstrated the consequences of sleep loss on attention. Most traffic accidents occur between four and six o'clock in the morning (and the middle of the afternoon). People without sleep feel tired and lane-drift, especially on monotonous roads. A study of American medical interns, published in 2005, found that the risk of a crash or near-miss was significantly greater if the medic had engaged in an extended, sleep-deprived work-shift. Experiments by Horne have shown that caffeine, listening to the radio and opening the vehicle window are poor at reducing sleepiness: the only successful way of doing this is to pull over and have a nap.

Lack of sleep does not affect us permanently – some of our behaviours are fine (physical activity, for example) and, if allowed to, we make up the sleep we have lost later. But memory, attention and cognition are affected in the short term. The brain seems to need slow-wave sleep in order to rest and recover: waking people up in this state leaves them groggy and confused. The brain also has two biological clocks which govern sleep – one controls circadian rhythms (those that change once a day) and is the responsibility of a brain region called the suprachiasmatic nucleus found at the bottom of the hypothalamus; another controls slow-wave and REM sleep.

People appear able to be categorised into evening-types (owls) and morning-types (larks). The former stay up later and wake up later and perform certain types of cognitive tasks better in the evening (whereas larks perform better in the morning). They also score higher than morning types on intelligence and creativity tests (on the downside, they are also more unstable and have more fractious social and family relations).

A note about dreaming

Paul McCartney once had a dream in which he heard a melody which he beat out on the piano when he woke up. The song, which he called 'Scrambled Eggs', became the most commercially successful song in history. The composition of 'Yesterday' is one in a long line of anecdotes attesting to the importance of dreaming for creativity and problem-solving. The mathematician Poincaré famously came up with the solution to a theorem that had plagued him for months, in his dreams. Dreaming is almost invariably produced in REM sleep – wake up people in this stage, and they will recall a dream and it will be a narrative (wake up people during slow-wave sleep and the dreams will involve situations rather than stories). That people dream indicates that they are not unconscious during sleep. There are Freudian explanations for why we dream, revolving around symbolism or repressed fear – ladies who dream of tree-trunks and rockets clearly have something specific on their mind – but these have little validity. Curiously, the REM sleep produced in dreaming reflects the movement of the eyes that you would observe if the person was actually acting out the dream. Thankfully, the paralysis seen in REM prevents a person from acting the dream out for real. In short, though, we have no idea why we dream.

Hypnosis

Hypnosis is different to sleep. Essentially a process whereby verbal suggestions are acted on involuntarily, the phenomenon was reported by an Austrian physician, Franz Anton Mesmer (hence mesmerism), in the eighteenth century. A person can be in a relaxed or active state when they are hypnotised but, normally, people will be given a suggestion to relax or fall asleep followed by suggestions to hand clasp ('you cannot separate your hands').

Hypnotised people are highly suggestible and the phenomenon in which hypnotic suggestions are acted out when not under hypnosis is called posthypnotic suggestibility. One theory of hypnosis argues that it reflects a different state of consciousness and that we have multiple systems of control which are not conscious at the same time: the hypnotist takes control of these. A competing theory argues that hypnosis does not reflect a change in consciousness at all, but more mundane phenomena such as compliance, role-enactment, conformity, and people's expectations. The power of suggestion and conformity (role-enactment and wanting to please the hypnotist) is great – in one study, when people who claimed not to be able to see the number eight were told that genuinely hypnotisable people could see this briefly, almost all participants claimed to see the number. The same researcher asked a group of hypnotised participants whether they could hear the 'experimenter'. They genuinely replied, 'no'.

Apart from its amusement value, hypnosis is psychologically useful because it can help people withstand pain. Some studies even claim that it is more powerful than morphine and tranquillisers – childbirth pain, dental drilling, and nausea brought on by chemotherapy can be helped by hypnosis (but only in hypnotisable individuals; the process also takes time). Hypnosis has also been found to improve the immune system functioning of students during stressful periods (exam time).

Various authors have sought to explain how hypnosis can conquer pain, but the mechanism is unknown. Some suggest that hypnotisable people can partition their attention more effectively – neuroimaging studies show increased blood flow in the frontal lobe and somatosensory cortex of susceptible people during hypnotic analgesia and the experience of pain. There may also be a placebo effect at work – one study found that although hypnosis helped people stop biting their nails, the best predictor of abstinence was a belief that the hypnosis would work.

4

Learning, remembering, forgetting

Learning

Languages, friendships, romance, work, all of these have one thing in common – they all require learning. Learning is the process that allows us to change our behaviour in response to experience, and psychologists have described (at least) two major ways in which we do this: classical conditioning and operant conditioning.

A considerable amount of our behaviour is a consequence of classical conditioning: the process by which we produce a response to a stimulus or an event because we have associated it with an event not previously related to it. Imagine blowing up a balloon in front of a child that had not seen an inflated balloon before. The balloon is inflated and inflated until it becomes over-inflated and bursts. Another balloon is inflated. Now, just as the balloon is getting to bursting size again, the child will flinch because it remembers the enormous, shocking bang that resulted from the previous over-inflation and suspects the same thing will happen again. The child has associated a previously neutral event (an over-inflated balloon) with an explosive event. The classically conditioned behaviour is the flinching.

The phenomenon of classical conditioning was initially observed serendipitously. The Russian physiologist Ivan Pavlov was researching glandular secretion and digestion in dogs when he discovered the famous association between the bell and salivation, described in chapter 1. In short, Pavlov presented food powder to one of his dogs which, naturally, salivated in response. Then, before giving the powder again, he rang a buzzer or bell. At first, the dog would just be startled but when given the powder, it would salivate. After a dozen or so pairings of powder and bell, the dog began to salivate when only the bell was sounded. The dog had learned that two previously unrelated stimuli had become associated. In the classical conditioning jargon, the food was the unconditional stimulus (because the dog would salivate to this spontaneously – an act called the unconditioned response) and the bell was the conditional stimulus (and the salivation becomes the conditional response).

Subsequent studies have found that, as Pavlov did, you usually need several pairings of the conditional stimulus and unconditional stimulus for a conditioned response to occur. Also, the intensity of the unconditional stimulus and the timing of the presentation of this and the conditional stimulus affects the likelihood of conditioning (the longer the delay between the pairing, the less likely the conditioning). Studies have also shown that when the conditional stimulus does not lead to a conditional response, conditioning is extinguished. So, if the bell did not always lead to the presentation of food, salivation to the bell alone would decrease. In addition, the conditioned response can recover spontaneously, a phenomenon that has echoes in real life. A novel unconditioned stimulus is more successful than a familiar one.

Classical conditioning is thought to be the mechanism by which we fear certain 'neutral' objects (a condition called phobia) or even hate and dislike them. One study from the 1960s found that people who had received an electric shock in the presence of another person (who had no part to play in the delivery of the shock) later acted in a hostile way towards that person, but not to another who was not present when they were shocked. The first human to be classically conditioned to fear a neutral object in an experiment was a healthy, nine-month-old infant called Little Albert. In the experiment, conducted by the great behaviourist John B. Watson and his assistant Rosalie Rayner and published in 1920, Little Albert was made to fear a previously neutral stimulus by exposing him to a repeatedly struck steel bar while an object (such as a rat) approached. Before exposure to the banging, Albert would approach the rat and cuddle it. When the noise and rat were paired, the presence of the rat alone later resulted in great distress: this fear generalised to other objects, such as a Santa Claus mask, five days later.

A second type of learning is instrumental learning or operant conditioning, pioneered by the American neo-behaviourist B. Frederick Skinner. Skinner originally wanted to be a writer (and, as a psychologist, actually wrote a successful novel, *Walden Two*, in which he translated his findings and theory of learning to fiction), but, instead, became one of the greatest psychologists of the twentieth century.

Operant conditioning involves learning through interacting with the environment. If we do something and we're rewarded, we repeat that behaviour; if our behaviour leads to less attractive consequences, we tend to indulge in less of it. The reward or punishment reinforces the behaviour and makes it more or less likely to occur again. Operant conditioning was first demonstrated by a hungry cat in a box, owned by an influential twentieth-century psychologist, Edward Thorndike. The cat had to learn that in order to escape from the box and get some food, it would need to activate a latch. At first, the cat would scratch around, meowing, pacing, and hissing. Once it had, accidentally, learned that the latch let it out, it subsequently learned to lift the latch the next few times it was put in the box, without the pacing and the meowing. A favourable outcome followed a correct response, a concept Thorndike called law of effect. It was like learning by trial and error.

Skinner took this a step further – in the process, changing the shape of psychology in the 1950s. Skinner's very experimental research usually involved an operant chamber – the so-called Skinner's box – an apparatus in which an organism such as a rat or pigeon could be observed and manipulated. Typically, a box would contain a lever which would dispense food, some lights and a speaker (it is largely due to Skinner's work that psychologists are associated with experiments with rats). Central to these experiments were the phenomena of positive reinforcement, negative reinforcement, and punishment.

Positive reinforcement occurs when the frequency of responding increases to a stimulus that we seek out. A simple example is going back to a restaurant whose food you like. Negative reinforcement occurs when the frequency of responding increases in order to avoid or end a stimulus which is unpleasant or painful. Burning yourself on a hot skillet and putting your hand under cold water is an example of negative reinforcement. Punishment is almost the opposite of negative reinforcement – here, a response is decreased by the presence of an aversive stimulus. For example, sticking your hand into the gorilla enclosure and having it bitten will probably teach you not to do that again. Punishment is often used to make animals and children learn and, in the short term, is effective. In the long term, however, it is harmful. It may be physically harmful (as when scolding a child; excessively this could border on abuse – the case of Genie in the next chapter is an excellent example), it may generate fear, loathing, retaliation, anti-social behaviour (children of physically and verbally violent parents are not violent at home but are with their peers), and other negative emotions in the person being punished. Perhaps more importantly, it only teaches a person what to avoid, not what to do. It does not teach desirable responses, only avoidant ones. A variation of punishment is response cost – a decrease in frequency of response that follows the termination of a stimulus. Imagine you're on a date. You're getting on well. Your companion is enjoying your company, laughing at your jokes, and showing an interest. Then, you make a disparaging remark about his/her favourite band. His/her smile evaporates. You rapidly move the conversation on to calmer waters. The removal of the smile has punished the disparaging remark.

We also learn through extinction – this is where a response is reduced because it leads to no reinforcement. A simple example is to stop knocking on a door because the reinforcer (someone opening it) does not occur.

Psychologists now generally distinguish between two types of reinforcement and punishment. Primary reinforcers are those to which we are biologically disposed to respond – food, water, comfortable temperature, rest, relieving an itch, having our genitals stimulated. Extreme cold or heat, cuts, blows, stings, a full stomach or bladder, and lack of air are examples of primary punishers. Punishers need not be deliberately applied – they can be any stimulus that prevents the likelihood of responding. Imagine that you're terribly unfit but are convinced by your lithe, athletic, enthusiastic friend that jogging for forty minutes will make you feel a lot better and fitter. You give it a go. The first few minutes, however, turn out not to be nice – the exertion and pain you feel make you conclude that they do not seem worth the effort. This is a punisher, but we can modify this by looking ahead to the potential benefits.

There are also secondary reinforcers and punishers. To a child, a ten-pound note is a little sheet of paper (in the same way that a clean wall is an open invitation to its inner artist) but, by seeing the note paired with a reinforcer (food, goods), the child will learn that it carries more significance (and learns that a clean wall is preferred that way for a reason). These are secondary reinforcers, as are smiles, praise, affection, and so on.

Various processes can affect reinforcement and, subsequently, the way we behave. Shaping is one. In Skinner's experiments, an organism's behaviour was shaped (in a fairly formal way) by making an outcome dependent on a specific behaviour. For example, a hungry pigeon would receive a pellet of food for facing the lever that operated the pellet dispenser, or when it approached the lever, or when it touched it. The pigeon learns that it will receive food only when it behaves in these ways. A real-life, human example might be praising a child for a poorly attempted drawing. As the child becomes more adept, and older, praise becomes dependent on a certain level of competence. Stand-up comedians hone their act partly through shaping (if they're successful) – they will try out material, ditching the unsuccessful parts that do not get a response and finessing the successful ones so that reinforcement (laughter, being liked) is achieved. Another form of shaping comes in the form of the Premack principle – the notion that the high probability of a behaviour occurring will reinforce a behaviour which has a low probability of occurring. For example, a parent may tell a child it can play with its bicycle (high probability behaviour) if it cleans its bedroom (low probability behaviour).

Underpinning all of the operant processes so far is the notion that reinforcement is presented after each response but we often don't respond immediately to a stimulus. In the romantic interaction above, for example, we would look like an idiot if we burst out laughing at every moderately amusing bon mot made by our companion. We would look bonkers. Sometimes, intermittent reinforcement is better (and, in this example, stops us looking rather mad, overly keen or very easily amused). This reinforcement follows what is called a ratio schedule: reinforcement only occurs after a certain number of responses have been made or after a period of time has elapsed. In Skinner's experiments, for example, a pigeon might only receive a pellet after five presses of the lever (not four, not six), or every tenth. If a reinforcer is produced after every tenth pressing, the pigeon rapidly learns that it will get food after the tenth press only and so pauses after the tenth pressing (this is a fixed-ratio schedule). An analogue in real life would be receiving a wage for producing or selling a certain number of items. A similar schedule reinforces but only variably – a reinforcer appears every three or thirty times, for example. Slot-machines make use of this type of reinforcer (called a variable-ratio schedule): the reinforcers are not predictable. Training can also make use of this schedule: a pilot undergoing training might be reinforced every time he/she succeeds at a task the first few times but, as he/she becomes more skilled, will only be praised every fourth or fifth time he/she succeeds.

We might also respond if a reinforcer appears after a certain length of time – for example, getting paid for working a week or a month, rather than for the number of goods we've sold or made (fixed-interval schedule). We might arrange to speak to a loved one at a certain time of day if they are working in another part of the country or world. At around the time of the call, we become a little excited, looking at the clock and phone, making sure that we've already eaten, picking up after the first ring, and so on. Like the ratio schedules, interval reinforcers can also be variable – in Skinner's experiment, a pellet would be dispensed to the animal after thirty seconds on one occasion, ninety seconds on another, and so on.

Of course, we can become resistant to intermittent reinforcement. Baldwin and Baldwin in their book *Behaviour Principles in Everyday Life* (where many of the examples here come from), cite the case of two girls, Connie and Paula. Connie threw tantrums regularly and the parents reinforced them; Paula also threw tantrums but her parents only reinforced her intermittently, about every six times (variable-ratio schedule). At school, the teacher disapproved of the tantrums and recommended the parents ignore them (extinction training). What do you think happened?

On the first day, Connie actually threw more tantrums, but this fell to zero in the following days. It took two to three weeks for Paula's tantrums to disappear. Why? Paula had become used to only intermittent reinforcement (every six tantrums or so) and so took longer to learn that her tantrums would not be reinforced at all. Connie had learned that her behaviour was not reinforced at all (she received no attention). The increase at the beginning was attributable to her thinking she had to produce more tantrums to get attention.

Some reinforcement is given only when high levels of responding are required – an athlete races to the finishing line, a business man rushes to meet a deadline for a bid, a policeman gets to the scene of a crime, or a builder uses quick-drying cement – or low levels – an artist takes time over a painting, a surgeon painstakingly removes a part of the brain, or a drinker learns not to drink too much too early in the evening.

Of course, learning can occur through other ways: modelling, for example (the adoption of a model as a way of behaving). Models can be real or symbolic (figures in books, films, television) and the way we learn from them is usually through observation. One study found that children who were afraid of dogs also had a parent who was afraid of dogs (even though the child had not directly experienced an unpleasant episode with a dog). Children's accents are learned through 'observation' and children are often explicitly taught other behaviours by watching their parents and teachers (and friends). In a new job, a person might observe how his or her seniors dress and consequently behave in and imitate that style. We might learn how not to behave by seeing a model punished (which dissuades us from engaging in that behaviour). We also fleetingly mimic others – if we're meeting a friend at a cafe for a chat, for example, we may not be that thirsty, but we might join our friend in a coffee anyway because she has ordered one. If we see people congregating around a shop window, we might be curious enough to join them.

A final note on observational learning. There is some evidence that when boxing prizefights are televised in the USA, the number of murders after the fight increases. What's more, if the loser is white, the number of white men murdered increases. If the loser is a black man, the number of black men murdered increases. A UK study examining the murder rates over sixty-three years found that the incidence of murder dropped after a well-publicised hanging (when hanging still existed as a sentence). This drop was seen for two weeks and then resumed to normal levels.

Memory

In the film *Memento*, the character played by Guy Pearce has to write on his body important information he had learned since his head injury, otherwise he would not be able to remember it. If he put notes in a diary, he would forget about them (and where the diary was). By writing on his body, he could be reminded because he could see the words reflected in mirrors. Pearce's character was based on a famous case study in psychology, HM. In the film, the character was unable to retrieve material after a head injury – a fate which also befell Dory in *Finding Nemo*; she could not recall names or remember where she was going.

The real HM underwent brain surgery to terminate the symptoms of epilepsy – this involved removing a part of his temporal lobe, including the hippocampus. This led to severe anterograde amnesia – the inability to learn new information (this contrasts with retrograde amnesia where a person cannot retrieve memories encoded prior to injury/surgery). He could not talk about anything that happened after 1953 (when the surgery occurred; HM was 27) but his memory before surgery was unaffected. His short-term memory is relatively unimpaired and he is aware of his memory problem. The deficit suggests that this part of the brain is necessary for the formation of new memories.

Cinema usually exploits artistic licence fairly flagrantly when dealing with memory loss, with consequences that science would probably like to forget (the two examples above, though, are notable exceptions). In films, loss of memory (or amnesia) is usually brought on by a bump to the head, for example (it isn't), and can be restored by another one (another no). In reality, the disorder is most commonly caused by neurosurgery or stroke. Fugue states, where people wander round only being vaguely aware of who they are, and personality change (à la *the Bourne Ultimatum*), are rarely seen in amnesic patients. Amnesia is the most common disorder resulting from brain injury and the most commonly malingered (where people feign the symptoms of memory loss). Most people who simulate amnesia, who usually do so to claim compensation for an imagined injury, will fail to remember their name, date of birth, home address and (in the USA) social security number, because they think amnesiacs do. In fact, people with amnesia can remember these reasonably well.

Without memory, there is no learning. Without it, we have no identity, no history, no knowledge of who we are. Memory is a process and not a unitary thing and there are different types of memory and different types of memory process. For example, we can remember visual or auditory material that has been presented for milliseconds (iconic and echoic memory), remember material for a short while but not permanently (short-term memory, STM), remember one thing while doing another, such as remembering a telephone number you have just being told, while dialling (working memory), and remember things learned a while ago (long-term memory, LTM). These are the processes of memory and there is evidence from psychology, neuroimaging, and brain injury to suggest they are distinct.

Some argue, however, that there is no distinction between STM and LTM and that these are points on a continuum. STM does seem to be limited, however, i.e. its capacity is capped. To illustrate this, take a look at the following numbers for about ten seconds. Then close your eyes and recite them to yourself. Then open your eyes again.

4, 9, 3, 7, 2, 8, 1

Now, do the same for these numbers:

8, 5, 1, 7, 3, 9, 2, 4, 8, 5, 2, 6

You could probably cope with the first set with ease but you probably found the second set trickier. The reason is that STM capacity is limited for certain types of information and we can usually store up to seven items plus or minus two. Material from STM reaches LTM probably as a result of rehearsal – the more rehearsal goes on, the more likely the material enters LTM (think of learning a times table or a song, or even a language). Sometimes, we rely on an interaction between different types of memory. If someone asked you to multiply seven by sixteen, for example, your sensory memory would allow you to hear the words, LTM would allow you to understand what multiply means (as well as the numbers seven and sixteen) but STM would allow you to hold all of this information 'in memory' to work out the answer. Here's another example. In the next five seconds, remember the following set of words:

cat, table, sexy, vegetables, car

Now, close your eyes and repeat them and once you've done that, open them again. Repeat the process for these words:

arp, prink, ozty, mitrablorin, olf

And, finally:

cath, bwrdd, rhywiol, llysiau, modur

You would probably be able to recall the first set perfectly, the second set not so perfectly and the third set not at all (unless you were a Welsh speaker; the words are translations of the English set). The English words are in LTM; the second set, being made up of pseudo-words, grammatically correct but non-existent words, could be partially remembered because we apply a system of rules (which we have in LTM) to reading and these words follow those rules (more on this in the next chapter). The Welsh words are, probably, unreadable – they are not in your LTM unless you hail from hen wlad fy nhadau (the 'Land of My Fathers' and, even if you did, you are probably sunk if you're from Cardiff).

There are also processes involved in creating memories – acquisition/encoding – and in remembering them – retrieval/recall and recognition. Retrieval involves freely recalling information unprompted from memory. Recognition involves, not unnaturally, the recognition of previously encountered stimuli that occur amongst other stimuli that had not been previously encountered. There are specific types of memory content. For example, we can remember and recall facts and figures such as how long it takes to boil an ostrich's egg (forty minutes, for the curious), what noises made up Tarzan's yodel (a camel's bleat, a hyena's howl, and a plucked violin), who was Prime Minister of the UK in 1973, and what the capital of Kenya is. These are examples of semantic memory. We can recall personally meaningful events or events that happened to us (autobiographical/episodic memory). We can remember how to do things, such as riding a bike or playing a piano (procedural memory). Psychologists have also singled out memories for public events that are shocking, vivid, emotionally and personally significant. These are the sorts of events which can trigger details of where we were and what we were doing when they happened. These are called flashbulb memories. Famously, the original flashbulb memory is John Kennedy's assassination. Other recent examples include the attack on the World Trade Center, the destruction of the Challenger shuttle, the death of Princess Diana, and the tube bombings of 7 July in London.

Psychologists have also distinguished between memories for events that we do not deliberately encode (implicit memory or learning without awareness) and those that we do (explicit memory). In one famous experiment, participants were exposed to six-letter words and asked to either think about these words or to judge whether they contained certain letters. They were then asked to recall as many of these words as they could, or were given the first three letters of the words and asked to come up with the first word that came to mind (this is a word–stem completion task). Those who had to think about the words recalled about forty per cent of the words when explicitly asked but only around five per cent when they judged whether the words contained certain letters. In the implicit condition (word stem), participants recalled around twenty per cent of the words, regardless of whether they thought about them or whether they contained a letter.

The two conditions in this study – thinking about words vs. searching for letters – reflect deep and shallow levels of processing (thinking about the words is deep) and these can influence retrieval. Deep processing involves elaborative rehearsal – forming associations to, and exploring the meaning of, the to-be-remembered material. Shallow processing can involve maintenance rehearsal – such as repeating words over and over again – or paying attention to superficial detail like the shape of letters in words. This type of processing is useful for learning material in the short term, but not the long term. Deep processing, which can arise from shallow processing, is what enables material to graduate from STM to LTM, where memory is thought to be consolidated.

Of course, deep and shallow are just words, and how they are defined depends on the author – they are best understood as metaphors for the idea they represent. That said, when students are divided into shallow learners and deep learners, the former are distinguished because they try to remember material; the latter because they try to glean meaning from material. When a group of students in one study is asked to read and summarise, in two sentences, a 1400-word article on curriculum reform in Swedish universities, you can probably guess which type of learner was best able to do this.

Another factor which can influence STM is the position of items in a to-be-remembered list. For example, we are more likely to remember words from the beginning and the end of a long list (phenomena called the primacy and recency effect, respectively). The explanation here is that the first words have entered a quasi-LTM store, whereas the last words are still in STM (because they were the last words we heard). If there is a delay between presentation and recall and we are occupied doing something else, the recency effect is abolished (presumably because this prevents rehearsal). That said, asking people to count from twenty backwards during the interval does not abolish either effect. Studies have also found that we can observe these effects for memory for opera attended over a quarter of a century ago, presidents of the United States, and parking positions. In 2002, a study of Methodist churchgoers' recall of the position of verses in a hymn showed exactly the same effect in semantic memory – they remembered the first and last verse but confused the order of those in the middle. Why? Perhaps items at the beginning and at the end are temporally distinctive: the more they are separated, the less likely they are to be confused with each other (and with those in between).

STM has its limits, as you saw when recalling the list of numbers above. It has temporal limits – one famous study found that if you prevent people from rehearsing for fifteen to eighteen seconds and have them do something else, recall can drop to zero – and it has spatial ones, summed up by George Miller's famous aphorism, 'The magical number seven, plus or minus two', which the exercise above exemplified. Of course, if this was all you could hold in STM, you would not be able to make sense of this and the author would not be able to get beyond tapping nine words or so. We can because we engage in 'chunking'– assembling together meaningful clusters of material. For example, take a look at the following sentences and see which ones you can most clearly remember:

1. Probably Highway my wouldn't it probably to name at you Charles think look me it is though
2. My name is Charles Highway, though you probably wouldn't think it to look at me

Because the second is arranged into meaningful clusters, we can remember it better (if you remember that this is the first line from *The Rachel Papers* by Martin Amis, your semantic memory is also magnificent).

We've seen that one way in which short-term memories are forgotten is by rehearsal prevention. Because STM is transient it soon disappears; it decays – rehearsal means it stays around a little longer. It can also be affected by displacement – because STM has its limits, new material will either be ignored or has to replace some of the material already remembered.

Remembering

When you look at these words on this page now, you do this fairly automatically. You do not pore over every curve and angle of the font, nor do you have any difficulty accessing the meaning of the words. So automatic is it that it is almost impossible not to think of a word when looking at it, as a phenomenon known as the Stroop effect demonstrates. In the Stroop task, colour words (blue, red, green, etc.) are presented in different colours (so the word blue is printed in red). The aim is to name the colour of the word. This is very difficult and most of us will struggle, first uttering the word itself rather than the colour it is printed in.

Remembering seems to be a reconstructive process. You've probably been on the receiving end of some gossip which, when the truth was finally uncovered, had a grain of truth but the details were inaccurate. Actually, this needn't be gossip – look at any twenty-four-hour news channel when an important breaking news story happens and see how quickly early established 'facts' later become non-facts.

One of the most famous examples of the creative nature of remembering was the Cambridge psychologist Frederick Bartlett's 1930s study of people's recollection of the short story, *The War of the Ghosts*. It was an unusual story about two hunters who got caught up in a tribal war. People were asked to recall details of the story just after reading it, twenty hours later and eight days later. Bartlett found that people did indeed engage in 'imaginative reconstruction' – on each occasion, they remembered the story a little differently. And in this, and other experiments, the more unusual the story, the more coherent and sensible the person's recollection tries to be – it was as if they were adjusting material according to their own view of reality.

A similar process is going on in this riddle: a lorry driver is travelling the wrong way down a one-way street but the police do not stop him. Why? When thinking about this, the key fact seems to be the lorry driving which is what we use to make sense of the riddle but this also makes it puzzling. Of course, the answer is that he was walking. We assumed he was driving a lorry because he was described as a lorry driver. The misleading nature of memory is famed. It is extremely brittle and extremely malleable, as the next section illustrates.

Unreliable memoirs

On 4 October 1992, an El Al plane lost its engine after take-off from Amsterdam Schiphol Airport. It returned to the airport but lost height and crashed into an eleven-storey apartment building. The event was widely reported in the news but was not actually filmed. Ten months later, a group of researchers questioned 193 individuals about the crash. When individuals were asked if they saw the plane hit the building, fifty-five per cent said that they had and fifty-nine per cent said that the fire started immediately on impact. In a follow-up study, sixty-eight per cent said they had seen the crash and sixty-seven per cent of participants said that they saw the plane hit the building horizontally (in fact, it hit the building vertically). The study, one of many, shows how memory can distort and how we claim to remember things we haven't experienced. Think about these phrases, for example, and identify exactly where they appeared: 'Elementary, my dear Watson', 'Beam me up, Scotty', 'You dirty rat', 'Play it again, Sam'. The obvious answers are Sherlock Holmes, Star Trek, and so on. Actually, none of these phrases was ever uttered.

In a series of now-famous and pioneering experiments in the 1970s, Elizabeth Loftus found that even the wording of questions asked about an event could alter people's memory of it. For example, if people watched two vehicles collide and were asked what speed one vehicle was going when it either 'hit', 'bumped', 'collided' or 'smashed into' the other vehicle, the more dramatic the verb, the greater the estimate of the car's speed. Even a small word such as 'the' or 'a' can distort our memory of events. Loftus asked people whether they saw 'a broken headlight' or 'the broken headlight' in a video of a collision. Twice as many people reported seeing damage when asked about 'the broken headlight' when no vehicle actually had a broken headlight.

When people were falsely accused of pressing the wrong computer key, the presence of an experimenter's stooge, who claimed to have seen the error, led a number of individuals to sign a confession saying they did. Another study found that if an experimenter's stooge reported seeing an object in a scene (it was not actually there), genuine participants also said that they remembered seeing it.

Loftus and others' research questions the nature of eyewitness testimony and eyewitness identification. In a review published in 1999, two of the most prolific researchers in the field argued that eyewitness identification in line-ups was the most common cause of a jury convicting the wrong person. Twenty-eight people were wrongly convicted based on eyewitness testimony in the USA in 1996.

Controversially, research on repressed or recovered memories (where a previously absent memory of child abuse, usually by the father, is uncovered through hypnosis or psychotherapy) indicates that there is little basis for the claims made. In one study of 930 cases of genuine sexual abuse, fifty-four per cent reported some form of sexual abuse before the age of eighteen and only 4.5 per cent reported abuse by fathers or stepfathers, a percentage which contrasts sharply with the incidence of paternal abuse in recovered memory cases. The more that people imagine a childhood event, the greater the confidence they have in believing the event had occurred. Perhaps this is one of the reasons why those who recover memories have such strong beliefs in events having taken place. In a survey of 1300 US registered psychotherapists, 300 doctoral clinicians and 300 chartered British clinical psychologists, ninety-four per cent agreed that it was possible for clients to develop illusory memories. Interestingly, most were confident that they could spot inaccurate memories in their own clients.

Research has shown that women who report recovered memories of abuse are significantly more likely to show false recognition – erroneously believing that a stimulus had been presented previously. For example, if a series of sweet-related words is presented and people have to recognise later which were presented in a series of sweet and non-sweet related words, such women were more likely to say they recognised sweet-related words that were not actually presented. They did not encode specific information but the general theme of the information, suggesting that those women who report recovered memories are more susceptible than other groups to developing illusory memories.

State/context dependent memory

Some types of material are better retrieved if the environment during encoding is the same as at retrieval. A study in the 1970s asked skilled scuba divers to remember a list of words in water or on land (yes, the 1970s were an unusual decade) and retrieve them either in the same or different environment. It found that participants recalled more words if the encoding and retrieval contexts were the same, whether land or water. This is called state or context dependent memory (the state part relates to the mood that you're in – so if you learn in a happy mood, you're likely to retrieve more in a happy mood and might retrieve more pleasant words than unpleasant; the opposite would be true if you were in an unhappy mood).

The life of a memory

How long does a memory last? One of the pioneers of memory research, Herman Ebbinghaus, tested this in 1895 when he learned sets of nonsense syllables (e.g. dax). He recalled much of this pretty quickly and even thirty-one days later could still remember some (but forgot most). In a more recent study, classmates were asked to remember as much information as they could about their peers, twenty-five years after graduation. The free recall of people's names and naming classmates' photographs declined over time – the further away from graduation, the less successful the retrieval (just as Ebbinghaus's was). Face recognition (rather than naming) and putting names to faces was quite good – ninety per cent got these right if they'd graduated within fifteen years (it declined after that). When the same researchers looked at second language learning at school, they found that retention of Spanish declined in the first six years, stabilised for thirty-five years and then declined again. This retention interval represented a 'permastore' that was impervious to forgetting. Similarly, studies of students' retention of a cognitive psychology course have found that knowledge retention declines in the first thirty-six months after learning but then stabilises. In all of these cases, the material that can be retrieved represents the remembering-to-knowing shift: material has not just been retrieved, it has been understood.

One factor that can disrupt LTM is interference. For example, more recently encountered information can interfere with what you already know (this is called retroactive interference), such as giving your new telephone number rather than your old one. What you already know, conversely, can interfere with what you have previously acquired, such as giving your old flat or house number instead of your new one or, Lord forbid, calling a new lover by an old lover's name (this is proactive interference). Memory for meaningful material, such as novels, is resistant to interference but one study recently found that people's memory for adverts was worse when these were embedded in a sexual or violent TV programme than in a neutral one.

I had that cabbie in the back of the scanner once …

The hippocampus, as you have seen, is a special little structure for memory. In the late 1990s, a study investigated the activation of the hippocampus in eleven London taxi drivers as they mentally navigated the shortest route between two points in the centre of the capital. The study found that the right side of the hippocampus was especially active when they did this (no activation was found when they had to identify landmarks or just recall sequences from famous films). While other studies suggest that activity is found just outside this area, it seems that the hippocampus is important for spatial navigation. A study of an experienced taxi driver with hippocampal damage found that he could orientate himself around a virtual reality version of London, locate landmarks and estimate distances between parts of the capital but he had difficulty in navigating roads that were not major arteries, suggesting that the structure is needed for understanding detailed, complex spatial relations.

It was a series of experiments in the 1980s with rats which demonstrated experimentally the importance of the hippocampus to spatial navigation. The animals were trained to find a platform in a container of milky water (so they couldn't see the platform). Eventually, they found this by trial and error. The rats then received surgery affecting the hippocampus, or the cortex, or no surgery at all. Those with damage to the hippocampus were extremely haphazard at finding the platform, whereas the other two groups found the platform relatively easily. 'Dwell time' was reduced, too: when the platform was removed, rats with hippocampal damage spent less time in the area where it used to be, compared with other rats.

Other regions of the brain are also involved in memory, as you would expect. Different parts of the frontal lobe engage in working memory: some are active during maintenance of material, others during manipulation of material. There is also some evidence that the left side is involved in encoding whereas the right is more involved in retrieval. Autobiographical memory encoding is associated with prefrontal lobe and temporal lobe activation. Greater EEG activation is seen during the successful encoding of learned words, i.e. EEG can be used to predict which words people recall successfully.

Sometimes, the brain fails memory. In patients with dementia of the Alzheimer Type, where protein deposits (some suggest it is Ab*56) in the brain cause a person to lose their memory and personality, there is widespread cortical atrophy, especially in the frontal and temporal lobes and the hippocampus and amygdala. A demented patient can't recall previously learned information, or retrieve autobiographical material from LTM; they forget rapidly, show poor attention, have working memory problems and show no primacy effect (but can show a recency effect). A.S. Byatt, reviewing Dame Iris Murdoch's last book, concluded that it was 'an Indian rope trick ... in which all the people have no selves and therefore there is no story and no novel'. Murdoch died shortly after and was found to have had Alzheimer's Disease. When the word use in one of her most successful books was compared with her last, her vocabulary was greatly impoverished in the last novel and high frequency words were much more common.

Dementia of the Alzheimer Type is the most common dementia (accounting for fifty per cent of all cases) and it has been estimated that five to ten per cent of people over sixty-five will develop Alzheimer's Disease. One study of centenarians found a 100% incidence, although others suggest that some centenarians may be impervious. Around twenty-three million people worldwide suffer from dementia, with diagnosis expected to double every twenty years. The cause is unknown although there is a familial form, carried on chromosome 21, and the E4 allele of the apolipoprotein gene is a risk factor for the disease and cognitive impairment.

5

Language and communication

Language: an introduction

From a gurgle to a smile, to *Finnegan's Wake* and *Bridget Jones's Diary*, we all try to communicate with each other in different ways. Language is humans' most successful medium of doing it. There are thought to be around 6000 languages in the world – Chinese is the most common, followed by English, Hindi/Urdu, Spanish and Arabic – but how would you define one? It is difficult to do but one way is to class it as any system of visual and/or vocal symbols that have meaning to the user and recipient. The study of these symbols, the rules governing their use, and the relationship between a language's structure and use, is called psycholinguistics.

Perceiving, producing, and understanding speech

Probably the second system of communication that we evolved was speech (gesture was most likely the first), around 250,000 years ago. Speech is produced in a continuous stream of sound. It is more versatile than writing: we can go up and down at the end of sentences, we can emphasise words, shout or whisper them, fill them with emotion, or we can … pause for effect (admittedly, that works for writing, too). As you saw in chapter 4, the primary auditory cortex helps us make sense of all of this.

Its role is to understand phonemes – the constituent parts of speech (these are not the same as letters – ship has four letters, for example, but only three phonemes: /sh/ + /i/ + /p/).

We probably recognise words as groups of phonemes. For example, in a study where a computer generated a synthesis of /g/ and /k/, people thought they heard kiss if the sound was followed by 'iss', and gift if followed by 'ift'. Speech also needs context: if people are asked to identify words isolated from an actual conversation, they can do this about forty-seven per cent of the time because conversation is full of sloppy pronunciation, muffled sounds and hesitations. If heard in context, they can identify them perfectly.

All languages have a syntax or grammar – a set of rules governing how we construct sentences. Like much of language, we learn syntactical rules implicitly and automatically. Some of these rules govern features such as:

- Word order – in English, as in seventy-five per cent of the world's languages, basic grammatical sentences tend to follow the subject-verb-object (SVO) order as in 'the boy hit the ball' (in Japanese it is S-O-V; in Welsh and Arabic, V-S-O).
- Word class – words that designate content (e.g. erotic, cooker, sprightly, rubber, etc.) are called content words (not surprisingly) and those that function to support content words (e.g. a, then, but, when, and, etc.) are called function words.
- Affixes – the endings we give to some words change their function in sentences – -ly, -ed, -ive, for example. In experiments where people recall sentences from invented languages, sentences with these endings are recalled better.
- Semantics – the meaning we derive from a sentence. This is especially important when the sentence is ambiguous, e.g. 'Having changed in the gym, Bill realised he had lost his trainer.' Did Bill lose his shoe? Or his fitness instructor?

All words are kept in a metaphorical store – the mental lexicon – which is accessed by auditory stimulation (either by hearing speech or reading text). Activating the word allows another region of the brain to assign meaning to it.

Famously, the linguist Noam Chomsky argued that we read or hear sentences in more than one semantic way. He proposed that there are three grammars. One reflects the rules that we use to generate the thoughts and ideas which produce the final grammatical form we want (generative grammar); the thoughts and ideas represent the deep structure; the final output is the surface grammar (e.g. speech). The brain allows us to translate what we mean at the deep level and produce it at the surface level.

It seems as if all languages share some common features – for example, (i) there is no real association between a word and the object it represents (the word dog, *chien* or *hund* has no meaningful association with the barking quadruped it describes); (ii) language is acquired through exposure to culture; (iii) humans can perceive and produce language. But there are, clearly, differences between individual languages. Interestingly, in one study, people found that speech coupled with appropriate gestures led to a better understanding of what the person was saying. In another, people increased the amount of representational gestures (those that carry meaning) if the recipient could not see their hands or face.

Language acquisition

Surprisingly, an infant can learn some aspects of language – such as discriminating between certain types of sound – before birth. The foetus can hear muffled sounds and many studies have shown that infants are more responsive to stimuli that they were exposed to in the womb (in one study, infants preferred to listen to a story that had been read by the mother while it was in the womb, rather than a different story). The infant's auditory system is well developed but, because it can't speak, psychologists have devised various methods of detecting the infant's attention to changing auditory stimuli. One is the suck response – infants will suck on a dummy or blanket more when they hear a new stimulus. Using this technique even one- to two-month-old infants can tell the difference between 'p' and 'b'.

The infant's response to speech, as well as its own speech development, follows generally predictable stages. For example, a newborn is startled by new noise, and will orient itself to it. At one to two months, it will smile when spoken to; at three to seven months, it will respond to different tones in speech (e.g. anger, happiness); at eight to twelve months, it responds to its name, to 'no', and recognises words it has been exposed to (e.g. 'peekaboo').

An infant's first vocal gesture is crying; this is followed by cooing (at one month). At around six months, its babbling begins to resemble the rhythm of speech (even as young as one to four days old, French infants prefer the sound of French; parents from different cultures can identify their infant from its babbling at six months). This influence of culture and context on the infant's development is important – one view argues that children have an innate ability to identify words of their native language. More recently, it has been suggested that what children can do is discriminate between rhythms of different languages – one study found that five-day-old infants could discriminate between Japanese and English (which are rhythmically different), but not English and Dutch (which are rhythmically similar).

In its first year, a child begins to speak – the first vowel is normally a soft 'a' and the first consonant a 'p' or 'b'. The next development tends to be nasality, where p and b morph into 'm'. At around eighteen to twenty months, the infant starts putting two words together. Because its vocabulary is small and its working memory limited, the infant's grammar is not the same as that of an adult. One suggestion is that the child has a language acquisition device which embodies the rules of 'universal grammar' – different languages will be slightly different but the basic grammar remains. Chomsky, for example, noted that adults' conversation with children is actually highly ungrammatical. If a child learned from this exposure, it would end up being as incomprehensible as Mr Bean. That there is a language acquisition device is not challenged – it is the brain and, up to a certain age, this can help us learn many languages (see below). Whether the device is so specific that it embodies specific universal grammar rules is not as clear.

The appearance of inflections and function words in children's speech, again, follows a general pattern – prepositions such as 'in' appear before plurals which appear before possessives. Adults' speech directed at infants tends to be short, well-formed and repetitive: pronunciation is exaggerated, few abstract words are used and words tend to be paired with objects and other tangible items the child can see. One study found that when mothers were asked to repeat how they spoke to their child, their reported language was much less simple than the actual interaction.

After the two-word stage, children begin to grasp the basics of adult grammar – object nouns are extended to noun phrases (e.g. 'that cat' becomes 'that big cat'). The use of verbs increases, articles are added ('a', 'the'), as are prepositions and then inflections (such as the past tense '-ed' or possessive ''s'). Inflections are not explicitly learned; the child picks these up from its interactions. Although they learn the past tense of irregular words first (they are more common), once children learn that regular words' past tense are formed with an '-ed', they generalise this rule to irregular verbs so 'came' becomes 'comed'. It is a few years before regular past tense order is restored.

One of the most efficient and obvious ways in which the child learns meanings of words is by having them paired with objects. The learning of content words is quick and the child is able to pick up words based on very few exposures – a process called fast mapping. The child will frequently overextend the use of words so they may say 'ball' when they see a ball, apple, orange or moon. Pronouns are difficult for infants to grasp, which is why parents' interactions usually refer to the infant's name (e.g. 'Does [infant's name] want teddy?' rather than 'Do you want teddy?').

Language and brain development

The development of language tends to be fairly relentless. According to the MIT cognitive psychologist Steven Pinker, 'there is virtually no way to prevent it from happening, short of raising a child in a barrel'. Tragically, some parents have raised their children, not exactly in barrels, but in similarly inhumane contexts. Genie, for example, was a young girl whose condition was only spotted accidentally at hospital where her mother was due for an appointment. She could not speak and, when she did, the words were limited to negative word pairs such as 'no more' and 'stop it'. The nurse thought she was about eight. She was four and a half feet tall and weighed around 25kg. She had nearly two complete sets of teeth. She was actually about to 'celebrate' her fourteenth birthday.

Genie had been exposed to horrendous child abuse. The girl's father had harnessed her to a potty in a room in the back of the family house since she was at least twenty months old. She slept in a crib which was covered with wire mesh. Her father was intolerant of noise and would beat her whenever she made any sound.

She could not talk properly and had a vocabulary of about 20 words (she could understand concepts such as 'red', 'blue', 'green'). A year after she was discovered, Genie's language ability underwent marked improvement. A young graduate student, Susan Curtiss, studied her after she was taken into care and tried to teach her the language she had failed to develop. By the end of this teaching, her ability to structure language using rules was the equivalent of a twenty-year-old's, she could tell the difference between singular and plural words and positive and negative sentences, and could understand some prepositions. However, while she made some progress, ultimately she had only achieved general language competence that you would expect of the most competent, taught primate.

Genie, and children like her, illustrate a fascinating property of language (and brain development). We seem to have a sensitive period for language learning – between the age of six and thirteen. Feral children – such as the Wild Boy of Aveyron who had his throat cut, was abandoned and was apparently raised by wolves – fail to learn language after a certain age. After thirteen, we have great difficulty in learning a new language. Aphasia resulting from brain injury in children is less severe and more recoverable than is aphasia in adolescents or adults. In fact, these children develop language almost normally. The reason is that during this time the brain exhibits 'plasticity' – it is still developing and so can accommodate discrete damage because another area will take over the disrupted function. The lateralisation of language tends to be complete by the age of ten years – speech will be localised in the left hemisphere in most children by then. (Astonishing as it may seem, children can have one hemisphere surgically removed and yet still function reasonably well.)

Can primates learn language?

Aficionados of 1980s British satire will be more than familiar with the *Not The Nine o'Clock News* sketch in which Mel

Smith's anthropology professor is being interviewed with his prize discovery and gorilla protégé, Gerald. The joke is that Gerald is equal to, and just as ineffably middle-class as, his mentor. The sketch spoofed scientists who aimed to humanise primates by teaching them language. Probably one of the most pointless endeavours scientists have undertaken is teaching primates language. An obvious question is: why would this be necessary? Even if it were remotely successful, it would only demonstrate an effect of training.

In the 1960s, there was great interest in whether primates could be taught language. Attempts at teaching speech had failed because chimps, for example, lack the control over tongue, lips and vocal chords that we have. Beatrice and Roger Gardner at the University of Nevada started a research programme that was to become quite famous: Project Washoe. Washoe was a female chimpanzee who was taught American Sign Language by the age of one. By four, she had learned 130 signs. She used two-word constructions (e.g. 'gimme flower'), sometimes extending this to three ('you tickle me'). When she learned the word 'open' she would generalise this to objects she would like to open. Washoe passed on the 'language' she had been taught to her male offspring. However, this process was slow and it is unlikely that she was learning language per se as rather than imitating and making connections between objects.

Another famous primate, a pygmy chimpanzee called Kanzi, was taught to communicate with humans by pressing symbols that corresponded to words. Interestingly, he also showed some understanding of human speech. In over 300 sentences uttered to him (almost all of the constructions had not been heard in that form by the chimp before), 298 were responded to correctly (e.g. he would follow the instruction 'Go to the refrigerator and get out a tomato'). Despite these intriguing results, however, primate language learning remained – and remains – rudimentary. No *Planet of the Apes* futuristic horrors just yet.

Reading

Reading is an artificial behaviour – we have to learn to do it (unlike seeing and hearing). The first writing system probably dates back to 4000BC Sumeria (present-day Iran and Iraq) and most likely reflected a need to keep accounting records of ownership of property. Most modern languages (Chinese is an obvious exception) use alphabetic writing systems comprising a few symbols (which represent sound).

When we read text, we scan – usually from left to right – making small jumps with our eyes (saccades) before fixating on certain words. We can actually measure these movements and see when they occur when people read – good readers make more forward saccades; poor ones, more backward saccades (because they re-read text). Familiar words tend to be skipped over, as are function words: one study of undergraduates found that they fixated on eighty per cent of content words and forty per cent of function words. Here's an example:

> I love Paris in the
> the springtime

You probably did not notice the second 'the' in the second line – we tend to glide over words like these.

The more unusual (and longer) the word, the greater the fixation time. In one study, people were asked to read two sentences about cinemas, one of which included the words 'cinemas must have adequate popcorn'; the other, 'cinemas must have buttered popcorn'. People dwelt longer on the former because 'adequate' is an unusual word to pair with popcorn. For this reason, people tend to spend longer reading *Ulysses* and *A Clockwork Orange* than they would *The Da Vinci Code*. The example also illustrates a concept called semantic priming – the idea that the presentation of one word can activate word-relevant memories that can affect later reading. For example, if the word 'horse' flashed on screen and you had to decide whether the next words (e.g. 'whip' and 'table') were real or nonsense words, you would respond more quickly to 'whip' because it had been semantically primed by the word 'horse' (the two, for better or worse, go together). Advertisers use this technique all of the time – when was the last time you heard an air-freshener described as 'dustbin drab' rather than 'alpine fresh'?

How do we read?

To make sense of what you see on this paper, you have to perceive and recognise the black marks on the page, then either recognise whole words or the component sounds of words. At first, as a beginning reader, we sound words out. We break and put together words (segmentation and blending), are aware of low-level physical features (we have limited sight vocabulary) and, importantly, we identify letters with sounds (a process called phonological awareness). As we become more experienced, we become more efficient.

When we encounter unfamiliar words, though, we have to sound them out, using what are called grapheme-phoneme correspondence rules. For example, when we see the word 'bast', we look at the individual physical components – the graphemes – and convert these into sounds based on rules we have learned (e.g. it looks and sounds similar to 'past', therefore we pronounce it to rhyme with 'past'). Other times, we do not need these rules – the word 'table' is usually recognised as a whole word because it is familiar. But there are exceptions. Take a look at this list: 'knave', 'shave', 'slave', 'have'. You were probably tempted to pronounce 'have' like 'slave'. This example highlights the importance of context in word reading.

The dominant model of reading suggests that there are two main routes from words on the page to understanding their meaning (it is called the dual-route model). The lexical route 'looks up' words in the mental lexicon to see if there's a match between the word read and the word in long-term memory; the sub-lexical route converts letters into sounds. The first route would be able to recognise all words we have already encountered; the second would be able to de-code regular words that are unfamiliar or that are non-words (e.g. flound). People with a certain reading disorder resulting from brain injury (phonological dyslexia), for example, can read whole, familiar words, but are unable to read grammatically correct non-words. Recent neuroimaging evidence suggests that these two pathways are represented by different systems in the brain.

The ways in which children learn to read broadly reflect these two routes – whole-word reading and phonics (although there are others). The latter involves teaching the child grapheme-phoneme correspondence rules, and has met with good success. Phonological skill is probably the most important predictor of good reading ability. The reading ability of poor readers who are taught to focus on the sounds of words by creating rhymes improves significantly. Reading ability also predicts later school success, including that in maths, reading and science performance.

Dyslexia

Dyslexia is a specific learning difficulty in which a person has extreme difficulty in reading. It can arise from brain injury (acquired dyslexia) or can develop despite normal intelligence and education (developmental dyslexia). The acquired dyslexias are rare, although they have helped shape theories of how we read, as we saw above. The estimated incidence of developmental dyslexia varies from 5 to 17.5%. Despite early evidence, boys seem no more susceptible than girls. Dyslexia often occurs in families and it is common for a male relative (usually, father) to be dyslexic. Dyslexic people can normally cope relatively well with life, and the list of successful people with dyslexia is impressive – Agatha Christie, Richard Branson, Michael Heseltine, A.A. Gill, Jay Leno and Danny Glover are only a few.

A fairly well-established feature of developmental dyslexia is poor phonological processing or awareness. The ability to segment words, an awareness of alliteration and the ability to execute linguistic operations (such as transferring the first letter of the words tomato and cucumber to make comato and tucumber; or saying what is left when you take the first or second sound away from a word) is impaired. Memory span for words and sounds is also poor. Various explanations have been proposed to explain the disorder. One argues that a visual pathway in the brain which carries information about space, depth and movement (the magnocellular pathway) is dysfunctional. A now famous neuroimaging study found that the area of the brain to which this pathway projects was not activated in participants with developmental dyslexia when they watched moving stimuli.

This pathway is also thought to act as an attentional spotlight, allowing us to filter out irrelevant information. When reading-impaired and non-impaired readers had to locate a stimulus in an array of other stimuli (e.g. a grey triangle amongst grey circles), the reading-impaired group performed less well as the number of distractors increased. Perhaps in developmental dyslexia there is an impairment in the ability to process stimuli globally.

At the neural level, reduced activation in parts of the temporal lobe have been observed in French, English and Italian dyslexic readers. Good reading ability has been associated with increased blood flow to a region called the angular gyrus. There is also a suggestion that one region of the temporal lobe – the planum temporale – is more symmetrical (equally sized on both sides of the brain; it is usually larger in the left hemisphere) in developmental dyslexia although evidence for this is waning.

A recent hypothesis suggested that the part of the brain responsible for motor function, the cerebellum, is dysfunctional in dyslexia because dyslexic individuals show lower activity in this structure when they execute novel and familiar motor movements. Reading involves a motor component, moving the eyes voluntarily and involuntarily, for example, and so perhaps a dysfunctional cerebellum contributes to reading difficulty. However, it is worth bearing in mind that the relationship could go in the other direction: the reading impairment could have produced the cerebellar dysfunction.

Other language disorders

On the morning of 30 July 1992, just before nine o'clock, Sir John Hale, the well-regarded art historian and prolific author, was found on his study floor, having the 'sweet witless smile of a baby' on his face and uttering only the words, 'the walls, the walls'. Hale had suffered a stroke. Sheila, his wife, had noted one of the signs just days before – a change in the musculature of his face. In her excellent book, charting her husband's illness, *The Man Who Lost His Language*, she records that immediately following his stroke, John Hale was unable to speak or write or match written/spoken nouns to objects such as a razor, a chick, a pencil, and some keys. He could surmise what people were saying from their gestures and tone of voice, would laugh at jokes and could follow simple instructions. Reading for pleasure was difficult and he would turn over pages he could not follow. Curiously, he could understand academic journals and offprints which suggested a dissociation between reading for pleasure and reading for information. Hale was showing the symptoms of aphasia. Remember from chapter 1 that some of the most important early discoveries in psychology were those of Broca and Wernicke, who reported that patients with injury to certain parts of the brain could either not produce speech or comprehend it. The total loss of language ability is called aphasia; the partial loss is called dysphasia, although aphasia is invariably used as shorthand for any sort of language loss.

In Broca's aphasia, a person's speech might be severely impaired; the patient produces agrammatisms – speech does not follow syntactical rules – as seen here:

Ah ... Monday ... ah Dad and Paul [patient's name] ... and Dad ... hospital. Two ... ah doctors ..., and ah ... thirty minutes ... and yes ... ah ... hospital. And, er Wednesday ... nine o'clock. And er Thursday, ten o'clock ... doctors. Two doctors ... and ah ... teeth. Yeah ... fine.

Patients seem to understand what is said to them and are often irritated and annoyed when they cannot express themselves vocally. That said, comprehension is not completely normal – they can fail to follow simple commands such as 'touch the red circle with the blue triangle', for example.

In Wernicke's aphasia, patients show poor understanding of speech and produce meaningless speech themselves, usually omitting content words. Here is an example where a patient is trying to describe a picture showing the theft of a biscuit:

Well this is ... mother is away here working her work out o'here to get her better, but when she's looking, the two boys looking in other part. One their small tile into her time here. She's working another time because she's getting, too.

Patients also fail to comprehend meaningful spoken instructions such as: 'point to the object with the ink in' (they will point to another object). Wernicke thought the region now given his name was where memories for sequences of sound that comprise words were stored. Brain injury is (psychologically) messy, however, and numerous deficits result from injury to Wernicke's (and Broca's) areas and the surrounding tissue (in fact, some researchers have suggested that you only see Broca's aphasia if there is also injury outside Broca's area). As any therapist will tell you, the clinical descriptions presented in journals become more haphazard in real-life interaction.

Damage specifically to Wernicke's area leads to a curious phenomenon called pure word deafness – people aren't really deaf and can hear sound but they have absolutely no idea what is being said to them; injury outside this area can result in Wernicke's aphasia but leaves the ability to repeat speech intact (it isn't in Wernicke's aphasia). There are various other aphasias and language disorders arising from brain injury (one is specific to the ability to name body parts, for example) and the further reading has more information on these.

Sex differences

The prolific American linguist Deborah Tannen has found some curious differences between men and women in the way they hold conversations and communicate with each other. Take the following example, from Tannen's book, *You Just Don't Understand*:

> A married couple was in a car when the wife turned to her husband and asked, 'Would you like to stop for a coffee?'
>
> 'No, thanks,' he answered truthfully. So they didn't stop.
>
> The result? The wife, who had indeed wanted to stop, became annoyed because she felt her preference had not been considered. The husband, seeing his wife was angry, became frustrated. Why didn't she just say what she wanted?

This, according to Tannen's research, sums up one important difference between men and women's language use: women often make a suggestion to start a negotiation. Men see it as a direct question to be answered directly. Another of Tannen's findings is that men's conversation can be a little like witnessing a verbal contest: it is a way of establishing dominance, not being pushed around, getting the upper hand. Women use conversation to encourage intimacy, closeness and support. Men are more independent, exemplified by a man's ability to make a unilateral decision which directly affects his partner without consulting her. Women try and win an argument by agreement – requests are formulated as proposals, not demands. Another difference is that men and women behave differently when dispensing advice and understanding – when a woman expresses a problem or difficulty, a man will suggest a solution, when what is usually desired is understanding and reassurance.

Whether men's and women's language is organised differently in the brain is currently unclear; some evidence suggests that women show greater bilateral activation during language tasks, other studies do not.

Sex is one important variable that can influence behaviour and is an individual difference, like personality and cognitive ability, that can affect the way we act, react and think. The next chapter considers individual differences, how they are measured, and what they mean, in more detail.

6

Individual differences: intelligence and personality

What is intelligence?

The Cuban Missile Crisis, the Iraq war, London's Millennium Dome, Suez, Coca-Cola's bottled water Danzai, self-cleaning underwear, *Gigli* ... these events and creations, and the decisions behind them, were presumably made by intelligent people (let's give the politicians the benefit of the doubt, for the moment) which begs the question: how did they arise? How could genuinely intelligent people make decisions that had such terrible – and predictable – consequences?

The decisions behind these examples illustrate beautifully the errors we make in reasoning, and these errors can be encouraged by other people, past decisions, predictions about the future, and having too little information available (or having too much). We'll come back to these at the end of this section and in the chapter on social psychology.

The answer, however, presupposes an understanding of what the word 'intelligent' actually means. We often use it synonymously with clever (when referring to a person) or creative and imaginative (when referring to a work of art). A survey by two psychologists of other psychologists' definitions of intelligence produced as many definitions as respondents. One of psychology's famous historians was more pragmatic: intelligence was whatever intelligence tests measured.

Theories of intelligence

What all psychologists agree is that intelligence describes a person's ability to learn, to remember, to recognise concepts and to apply information we have learned to adapt to our environment. Psychologists generally distinguish between two types of intelligence – fluid and crystallised. Fluid intelligence represents innate ability; crystallised intelligence represents what has been learned (e.g. knowing how to fuse a plug, play a piano, who wrote *The Dubliners*, and so on). The distinction was made by Raymond Catell in the 1950s based on a procedure called factor analysis. Factor analysis is a statistical technique used to identify a common factor or theme underlying various scores on tests. For example, on a personality test, five or six statements may be highly correlated (if you scored highly on one, you would score highly on the others), suggesting that the sentences may measure the same general factor or theme (extraversion, say). Of course, factor analysis can't give absolute descriptions of intellectual ability – the names given to the factors are determined by the investigator to begin with, so there is an element of subjectivity in the process.

In 1927, Charles Spearman suggested that our intellectual ability is based on a general intelligence factor (called 'g') and another factor specific to performing successfully on certain intelligence tests (called 's'). There is much to commend this: when given tests of intellectual ability, people's scores do correlate, suggesting that there may be an underlying factor common to all. Some tests correlate more highly than others, suggesting a more specific ability (visuospatial ability, for example). Spurred by this finding and this theoretical approach, psychologists went about conducting factor analyses of data from various intelligence tests (more on these below). But back to Cattell. Another psychologist called Louis Thurstone gave a series of fifty-six tests to undergraduates and found that these tests could be reduced to seven factors, e.g. verbal comprehension, verbal fluency, memory, and so on. When the data were re-analysed, Cattell found two factors which could account for the data reported by Thurstone: these were fluid and crystallised intelligence.

These aren't the only major theories of intelligence, however. In the 1980s, the American psychologist Robert Sternberg suggested that intelligence comprised three components: componential, experiential, and contextual intelligence. This triarchic theory of intelligence goes beyond traditional intelligence test factors to include practical aspects of behaviour. The first component represents the mechanics we use to plan and execute behaviour; the second allows us to deal with novel situations and to solve problems previously encountered; the third component reflects the skills that were subject to natural selection (fitting in, developing appropriate skills, finding a niche for oneself).

A second major theory is Martin Gardner's multiple intelligences. Based on neuropsychological data, and superficially similar to Thurstone's, the theory suggests that there are at least seven types of intelligence: linguistic, logical/mathematical, musical, spatial, body/kinetic/kinaesthetic, interpersonal (awareness of others' feelings) and intrapersonal (awareness of our own feelings). The first three are not unusual – psychologists had already agreed that these could exist; the last four, however, are unusual. As this section demonstrates, there continues to be vigorous discussion over the nature of intelligence.

There is another, unrelated, concept called 'emotional intelligence' which refers to the ability to empathise with others and interact socially, but its status as a separate type of intelligence is questionable – it may comprise two factors, for example, social skill and emotional skill. The first correlates well with successful interview performance.

Intelligence testing

The most widely used intelligence 'test' in the world is the Wechsler Adult Intelligence Scale, originally devised by David Wechsler in 1955 as a means of screening soldiers in the US army and revised twice since (the last time in 1997). The WAIS is a battery of fourteen tests that have been validated on 2450 people from thirteen age groups and is relatively culture-free (this was a criticism of previous versions). There are even Scottish and Welsh versions. The tests measure two factors: verbal intelligence (verbal IQ) and non-verbal or performance intelligence (performance IQ). This test is what gives us the IQ (intelligence quotient) – the two factors are combined to give a score. Subtests of the verbal scale include tests of:

- information (e.g. what is the capital of France?)
- comprehension (practical reasoning/interpretation of proverbs)
- similarities (abstraction and verbalisation of properties common to objects)
- arithmetic reasoning
- digit span (repetition and reversal of numbers presented aurally)
- vocabulary (definitions)

Subtests of the performance scale include:

- digit symbols
- picture completion (identification of missing features from line drawings)

- picture arrangement (arrangement of cartoon pictures in a meaningful order)
- block designs (constructing a pattern with blocks from a given design)
- object assembly (timed construction of puzzles)

The average score is 100. Intelligence, like height, is normally distributed – that is, if you plotted everybody's height and IQ score on a graph, the line would look bell-shaped with most people falling in the middle range, representing average height/intelligence, and the others occupying the tails (very short/low IQ; very tall/high IQ). Just over sixty-five per cent of people, therefore, would score between 84 and 116 IQ points; only 0.13% would score between 36–52 or 158–174.

It wasn't the first – and isn't the only – intelligence test. Even in 2200BC, Chinese authorities assessed the performance of civil servants (mandarins) in a manner similar to modern psychometric tests. There are hundreds now available, measuring various abilities such as creativity, vocabulary, spatial reasoning, etc. They are sometimes controversial because of what they might imply and because they may affect whether we get a job. The precursor to modern intelligence tests was Alfred Binet's scale. Binet was a French psychologist who was asked to devise a test to see which children could benefit from special classroom instruction (like Wechsler's, therefore, it was not originally devised as an intelligence test). With Theodore Simon, he devised the measure in 1905. The scale allowed assessors to determine a child's mental age – the level of achievement that would be expected for an average child – and a child scoring better than expected for his or her age would have a mental age several years higher than his/her actual age. The test was translated in the USA about ten years later and contained the formula for calculating IQ:

mental age/chronological age × 100

Our test scores have been improving, decade on decade, since 1930 – people living then would have an IQ generally thirty points lower than someone living in 2000. One Dutch study in the 1990s found an eighteen to twenty point jump in a generation. The reason is probably better education – especially elementary education – and an emphasis on teaching cognitive skills that underpin fluid intelligence. Although there is a relationship between job success and IQ, there is no meaningful correlation between high IQ and greater income.

Sex differences

Probably, the third most controversial topic in intelligence (after the role of genes in intellectual ability, and the validity of intelligence tests) is whether men and women (and boys and girls) differ on tests of intelligence. We know that our perception of a person's intelligence is affected by our sex and the sex of the person we're judging. Daughters and sons rate their father as more intelligent than their mother and both parents regard their sons as being more intelligent than their daughters. A study of Hawaiian, British and Singaporean respondents, by Adrian Furnham and myself, asked people to rate themselves on each of Gardner's intelligences. We found that men judged their mathematical and spatial intelligence much more highly than did women. This is not a surprising finding given what we know from research on sex differences in performance. For example, Diane Halpern summarised some of the reported sex differences in specific abilities – where women score higher than men, and men higher than women – in her *American Psychologist* article in 1999. The only sex difference to be reported consistently and reliably over the past three decades is visuospatial ability – specifically, the ability to rotate objects mentally in three-dimensional space. Men are much better at it than women. Figure 12 shows

(a)

(b)

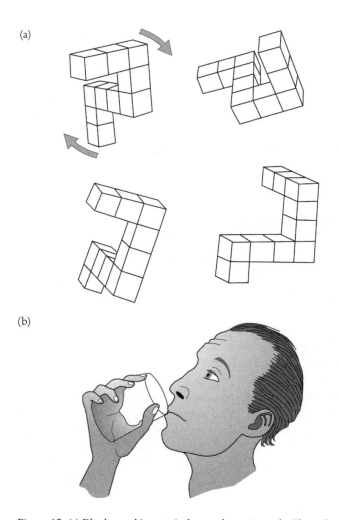

Figure 12 (a) Blocks used in a typical mental rotation task. The task requires you to indicate whether the rotated set is the same as the target set (but differently oriented); (b) The water level task. The task requires participants to place a line in the glass where they believe the top of the water should be. On average, men are better at estimating this than are women.

a couple of examples where men's performance excels that of women.

Why should this be? Some have suggested a biological basis – men occupy more professions, and study more degree subjects, that rely on spatial reasoning and mathematics, and the amount of testosterone correlates with spatial ability (although the evidence is not consistent). Evolutionary theories reflect the hoary old cliché of hunter-gatherer but more sophisticated interpretations might be quite plausible. For example, in 2004, two psychologists proposed that, although there are spatial intelligence differences between men and women, each is better at certain types of spatial skill. Women do outperform men on some visuospatial tasks – visual recognition, for example. In evolutionary terms, women are better at navigating and making decisions about the proximal environment (harking back to the day when women were left to raise children and did not stray from the homestead, while the men hunted); whereas men are better at large-scale navigation (because they had to go out and roam and hunt). There is some modern evidence to support this. When asked to give directions, for example, men give detail about distance and direction, but women are more likely to use landmarks. Academically, boys are either likely to perform exceptionally well or exceptionally badly. As the evolutionary psychologist Helena Cronin put it, with boys there are more dumb-bells but also more Nobels.

Another interpretation of sex differences, suggested by Simon Baron-Cohen, is that men and women differ in terms of information processing style: they either empathise or systemise. In the first, people work at identifying someone's thoughts and feelings (perspective-taking, altruism, co-operativeness); in the second, they analyse relationships in non-social interactions (showing an interest in science, technology, the natural world, etc.). Women are thought to be better at the former; men, the latter. In a recent study, men were found to engage in higher levels of systemising than were women, and non-heterosexual women showed higher levels than did heterosexual women. There were no differences between heterosexual and non-heterosexual men. Women did show a greater interest in the arts and culture, however, which may not be related to sociability/empathy.

On the topic of spatial ability, some controversial research published in the early 1990s claimed that listening to ten minutes of a Mozart sonata was associated with significantly better performance on some spatial tests compared with exposure to ten minutes' relaxation or silence. On the basis of this and other research, newborns in the US state of Georgia were baptised to the sound of Mozart, in the belief that the strains of the genius composer might enhance their mental machinery. However, a good sign of a robust phenomenon is its ability to be replicated and studies since have not supported the original research – it seems that music similar to Mozart (and music that increases positive mood) can produce benefits, but only on specific tasks.

Heredity, environment and intelligence

The argument over whether environment or genes determines intelligence (the nature–nurture debate) is more or less dead and buried and has been for a while. Both are important: the focus is currently on how the variation in each influences intellectual development. The environmental component seems self-explanatory – a happy, encouraging home, good schooling, appropriate education, and so on, help cognitive development. The genetic component is much more complex.

The statistic that refers to the degree of variation in intelligence attributable to genetic variability is called heritability. Two ways of determining the relative contribution of each – at least in a crude way – is to measure the IQ of dizygotic or fraternal twins (fertilised from different eggs) and monozygotic or identical twins (fertilised from the same egg; they are, therefore, identical) and that of children from biological and adoptive families. In one study, the correlation between the IQ of biological parents and their offspring (who had been adopted) was higher than that between the offspring and their adoptive parents, indicating that having a shared environment contributed less to intelligence than did genes (the only exception was for vocabulary, a facet of crystallised intelligence). Similar results have been found for tests of verbal and spatial ability in identical and fraternal twins – across the lifespan, the IQs of identical twins remain more similar (even in old age). When identical twins are reared apart, their scores – although less similar than identical twins raised together – are more similar than fraternal twins reared together.

When the contribution of environment is considered in intelligence studies, it usually accounts for about twenty-five per cent of variance, i.e. the percentage of intelligence attributable to environmental factors is twenty-five per cent (some suggest it is much lower). Why? The behavioural geneticist Robert Plomin suggests that these estimates are low because the environment in a family is not the same for every family member. Although there may be the same number of books on the bookshelf, the same number of trips to the theatre or museum, etc. in the shared home, children are not treated identically by their parents and family members. They might look different, have different personalities, have different interests, etc. The environmental contribution to intelligence is actually larger in childhood than adulthood – probably reflecting the fact that there is more of a shared environment but, when children have flown the coop, their different environments shape them differently. One study found that the percentage of intelligence attributable to the environment drops from thirty per cent to three per cent in adulthood.

If intelligence has a genetic component, what is it?

Plomin and his colleagues have made an extensive study of DNA markers – enzymes used to locate parts of DNA – from Caucasian children of varying intelligence, from low IQ (less than 59) to high IQ (over 142), and have found small differences in DNA between those with low and high IQ. Several of the 100 identifiable DNA markers have been associated with intelligence, but no one marker has been consistently associated with it. A recent study has located a DNA marker for the gene on chromosome 6 which appears with greater frequency in a high IQ group (IQ over 136) than a control group (IQ = 103). This is an exciting finding because it was replicated in a group with even higher IQ (over 160). The researchers caution, however, that the gene accounted for only a small portion of the genetic influence on intelligence and that many more genes may be implicated. Nonetheless, this new area of research may hold the key to identifying the genetic basis of intelligent behaviour.

Possibly the most controversial topic in psychology centres on race and intelligence. In October 2007, London's Science Museum hastily cancelled a talk by Nobel Laureate, James Watson, because of views he expressed in a British national newspaper about the intelligence of Africans and Westerners. At the time of writing, his employer (The Cold Spring Harbor Laboratory) has suspended him from duties. A now famous book, *The Bell Curve*, written by a sociologist and a psychologist, caused a stir when it appeared in 1994 because it concluded that a general intelligence factor exists, intelligence could be measured by IQ tests, IQ was genetically determined, and racial differences in IQ were the result of heredity. Many studies have established that there are racial differences in scores on various tests of intellectual abilities. People who are identified as black generally score an average of 85 on IQ tests, whereas people who are identified as white score an average of 100. Although many black people score better than many white people, on average whites do better on these tests. Lynn's study of 2260 children between six and seventeen years of age found that Asian children scored an average of 107 IQ points, white children an average of 103 and black children an average of 89. Black infants are more advanced than their white counterparts in the first fifteen months of life. The controversy, however, lies not in the findings themselves but in what these findings mean. Some authors have argued that the racial differences in scores on the tests are caused by heredity, and *The Bell Curve* highlights the failure of intervention programmes to improve the IQ of black children.

However, a study by Scarr and Weinberg found evidence that environmental factors could substantially increase the measured IQ of a black child. Scarr and Weinberg studied 99 black children who were adopted into white families of higher-than-average educational and socioeconomic status. The expected average IQ of black children in the same area who were raised in black families was approximately 90. The average IQ of the adopted group was 105.

When we point to group differences in races we are referring to general, average differences in intellectual performance; there are considerable within-group differences which may even be larger than between-group differences. There is also a problem with what we mean by race. We can define race biologically by gene frequencies or we can define it as a social construct. For many people, race is whatever they believe it to mean; they themselves ascribe meaning to it. In this sense, the concept of race makes very little scientific sense.

Creativity

According to the novelist Victor Hugo, creativity is intelligence with an erection. Setting the unsettling imagery aside, is it clear that creative thinking and output are characterised by intelligence and excitement and originality. Like intelligence, however, creativity has been difficult to define satisfactorily. A work of art or a novel or a bridge or a pop song (even one by Chikinki) is a creative output but so is a mathematical formula or a child's construction out of blocks. The important thing about creativity is that it has an original output.

In the laboratory, one of the most widely used creativity tests has the participant creating as many uses for a simple geometrical shape (a circle, say) as possible. Another asks for a list of similarities between words. Some research suggests that creative people are flexible risk-takers and are open to experience. They have skill, a certain cognitive style, and a motivation to create. They may show high levels of psychoticism – a cold, manipulative and indifferent personality style – but data on this are inconsistent.

A considerable body of research suggests that creativity is closely allied to psychopathology – in Dryden's words, 'Great wits are sure to madness near allied, and thin partitions do their bounds divide'. Studies have shown that the incidence of mental illness is especially high in creative men – depression has been found in a majority of great writers, and jazz musicians of the 1920s and 1930s. Some research has found that parental conflict is associated with greater creativity in children and a study published in the *Journal of Personality and Social Psychology* in 2006 found that even thinking of a potential, attractive partner increased creativity, but only in men – women only showed increased creativity when thinking about a trustworthy or committed potential partner. These findings seem to support Igor Stravinsky's belief that 'in order to create, there must be a dynamic force — and what force is more potent than love?'

Reasoning and decision-making

Humans are natural problem solvers — evolution has made us so. From building houses and bridges, to hostage negotiation, to performing heart surgery, to growing food, to completing crosswords and the Rubik's cube, we apply our talents to all sorts of problems. When we reason, we infer something by adopting general principles or rules or applying logic (deductive reasoning) or we can infer general principles from specific examples (inductive reasoning).

An example of the first would be a syllogism — a form of logic invented by Aristotle. It begins with a major premise, followed by a minor one and a conclusion:

> Norman is taller than Nigel.
> Natallie is shorter than Nigel.
> Therefore, Norman is taller than Natallie.

Some syllogisms may lead to conclusions that are incorrect and we have to decide whether they are logical or not, e.g. 'My dog has four legs; my cat has four legs; therefore, my cat is a dog'.

Some psychologists have argued that the ability to solve syllogisms is related more to our spatial than verbal ability and that we create mental models — mental constructions based on reality — when we read each statement. A well-known (at least, in the psychology laboratory) example of inductive reasoning is a task in which a person sorts cards according to the type, number or colour of pattern on them. The participant infers which criterion is correct from feedback given by the experimenter and he/she eventually learns the rule. If the rule is changed, without explicit awareness by the participant, patients with damage to an area of the frontal lobe cannot learn that the rule has changed. In fact, neuroimaging and brain injury evidence suggests that the frontal lobe is involved in reasoning and decision-making. One hypothesis suggests that the frontal lobe, if disrupted, allows us to engage in risky behaviour, such as gambling large sums of money, because we are not aware of the bodily sensations associated with risk (increased heart rate, for example) which the frontal lobe would usually allow us to detect. Detecting such changes usually makes us aware of how risky our behaviour might be and prevents us from engaging in that behaviour.

'To err is human ...'

... and never is this truer than in the realm of reasoning. We commit errors of reasoning frequently and they can afflict the most prestigious institution, company and government and the lowliest citizen, as the examples in the opening of the chapter illustrate. The next section describes some errors in reasoning that psychologists have demonstrated in decades of research. Many of the examples here come from Stuart Sutherland's excellent book, *Irrationality*.

Availability error

Are there more words with 'r' as the first letter or as the third letter? While you're thinking about that, are there more that begin with the letter 'k' than have 'k' as the third letter? If you answered 'yes', you have committed an availability error. We tend to think there are more words beginning with 'r' because these words are readily accessible or available to us and are organised in our 'minds' in this way. Here is another example.

One study asked participants to indicate how many men's and women's names had been presented in a list of famous and fictitious names. When the lists contained names such as John Kennedy and Winston Churchill, people thought there were more men in the list (there weren't); the same thing happened when famous women's names were included. These made more of an impact because they were available to us. A similar phenomenon is at work when we feel persuaded that an item costing £5.99 is much cheaper than one priced £6.00 (the '5' is made more available); and when we fear flying because of a recent terrorist atrocity. In the 1980s, Americans were reluctant to fly because of a fear of hijacking following well-publicised incidents. However, one 1986 study found that Americans were more likely to die a violent death in their own city than when flying.

Halo effect

One coherent, available, positive trait can cloud our judgement of people. For example, we tend to rate handsome men and beautiful women as more intelligent, athletic and humorous (although there is no evidence that they actually are) than less attractive people. A very devious study in the 1980s sent psychology articles that had already been published, to the same journals they were published in but the names and affiliations were changed – authors from very prestigious departments (e.g. Princeton) were changed to those from invented, more lowly, institutions. Eight of the nine papers were rejected by the journals that had originally published them.

A similar fate befell one of Jane Austen's novels submitted, mischievously, by an organiser of an Austen festival, to literary agents and publishers in 2007. None accepted the manuscript. Only one recognised it. The absence of Austen's beatific halo made respondents treat it as any old novel. However, the converse can happen. The perception of one negative trait – selfishness, for example – can sour our impression of another (the devil effect) and we'll come back to this in chapter 8.

Confirmation bias

We tend to reason in a way that confirms what we already know rather than in a way that will teach us something new. This is called the confirmation bias. In this sense, the exception never proves the rule – an exception proves the rule is wrong (the original proverb actually stated 'exception tests the rule', which is correct).

Sure thing principle

If we prefer A to B in all states of the world, we should prefer A to B in any state. But it is not so. One study asked students to imagine they were waiting for exam results and to decide on whether to book a holiday immediately or defer the decision and place a deposit only after knowing the result. Those who were told the result booked the holiday regardless of whether they passed or failed. Those who were not told, deferred, although they said they would book the holiday whether they passed or failed. Why, therefore, defer?

Probability heuristic

A fancy name for a common mistake – drawing conclusions based on what we believe rather than on reality. Take a look at this exercise:

Linda is thirty-one years old, single, outspoken and very bright. She graduated with a degree in philosophy. As a student, she was deeply concerned with issues of discrimination and social justice, and also participated in anti-nuclear demonstrations.

Please rank the following by their probability, using 1 for the most probable and 8 for the least probable.

A   Linda is a teacher in primary school
B   Linda works in a bookstore and takes yoga classes
C   Linda is an active feminist
D   Linda is a psychiatric social worker
E   Linda is a member of Women Against Rape
F   Linda is a bank teller
G   Linda is an insurance salesperson
H   Linda is a bank teller and is an active feminist

So, how did you do? If you answered like the participants in the original study you would be less likely to think that Linda was a bank teller than a bank teller and a feminist. Bank tellers, apparently, do not make good feminists (or are not known for being feminists). But this ignores the principles of probability. If people are told that 100 people fit the description they have read and asked how many are bank tellers/feminist bank tellers, the error is reduced.

Failure to utilise a comparison group

Say you were told that Drug A made seventy-nine per cent of a study's respondents better. Would you accept that Drug A was magnificently effective? You probably shouldn't because you need more information. Did the study use a control group of people who received no drug and a group that received a placebo (a sham drug that looks and feels like the actual drug but has no pharmaceutical value whatsoever)? A related error is the failure to utilise base rate information – for example, stories in newspapers about single mothers who exploit the welfare system might lead people to think that there are more exploitative single mothers than there actually are. Similarly, parents who refused to inoculate their children against mumps, measles, and rubella because of one, poorly controlled, tendentious, unreplicated research paper linking the vaccine with autism also committed an error of reasoning, with slightly more significant consequences.

Sunk cost error

Before his election as Prime Minister, Tony Blair boldly declared that the first line of the 1997 manifesto would be about the building of the Millennium Dome in London. This curate's egg of an exhibition – part worthy education, part entertainment, designed to be open for one year (2000) and housed in a magnificent canvas dome in Greenwich – was one of the Labour government's most commercially disastrous projects in its first term. Many came – it was one of the UK's most successful tourist attractions, in terms of numbers visiting – but not enough to meet its projected visitor numbers (and, therefore, not enough to ensure its independent financial health). No matter how much money it consumed, more was ploughed in simply to keep the exhibition going, and still the numbers visiting did not significantly increase. This is an example of the sunk cost error – a refusal to abandon a basket-case project because too many resources have already been committed. The government did not – perhaps could not – capitulate and close the project. The loss of face would have been too embarrassing and too much money had already been spent.

The slide

We can often be convinced to make decisions we do not agree with. The salesman's foot-in-the-door technique is one way that can lead to this – people can be gradually persuaded to do something else because they have already agreed to do something. For example, a 1966 study asked Californian house-wives to put up a 'Be a safer driver' sign. Later, they, and a previously unapproached group, were asked to erect another, hideous driving safety sign. Three-quarters of those who had already agreed to have the first sign erected agreed to accept the second; only one in six of new respondents did.

We'll come back to other biases in chapter 8.

Personality

'My theory is – we don't really go that far into other people, even when we think we do,' says a character in Martin Amis's novel, *Other People,* 'We hardly ever go in and bring them out. We just stand at the jaws of the cave, and strike a match, and quickly ask if anybody's there.' A major way in which we differ from another, psychologically, is in our personality. Personality is a pattern of behaviour or thinking that is consistent across most situations and across time and which helps distinguish one person from another. There are currently two major approaches to studying personality; one is more scientific than the other. We'll describe the scientific approach first.

Trait theories

Back in the second century BC, the Greek physician Galen proposed what was probably the first trait theory of personality.

The body was thought to contain four humours (fluids) – yellow bile, black bile, phlegm, and blood. A person would have more or less of each fluid, which would influence his/her character. So, a choleric person would exhibit an excess of yellow bile and was short-tempered, a melancholic person would exhibit an excess of black bile, and so on. In the strictest sense, however, these were not traits – enduring personal characteristics – but types. Modern characterisations see people as not falling into categories but as possessing a trait to various degrees (so, some people will vary on the trait of 'outgoingness', rather than being classed as outgoing or not outgoing).

One of the first modern, scientific attempts to define core personality traits was undertaken by Gordon Allport who identified all words in a dictionary that pertained to personality (18,000 of them). He then attempted to see whether certain words could be clustered together to form a trait – 'bashful' and 'shy', for example. The next major development was Cattell's approach, which used Allport's list of adjectives as well as interviews with people. He identified sixteen traits upon which personality was built (e.g. cool–warm, affected by feeling–emotionally stable, shy–bold). A third significant approach was taken by the British psychologist Hans Eysenck, who used factor analysis to identify three core personality traits or factors: introversion–extraversion, neuroticism–stability, and self-control–psychoticism. A person would fall along a point on these three continua, as measured by a questionnaire. An extreme extravert, for example, would be very outgoing; an extreme introvert would prefer solitary activities; an extreme neurotic would be anxious and full of worry; an extremely emotionally stable person would be relaxed; an extreme psychotic would be aggressive, egotistical and anti-social; and a person with extreme self-control would be kind, considerate, obedient of rules.

An important facet of Eysenck's approach is that these traits are thought to be grounded in biology, specifically brain activation. Introverts have high levels of arousal, indexed by 'cortical excitement' and, therefore, do not behave in a way that would cause additional arousal; extraverts, on the other hand, have low internal arousal, and need additional stimulation to reach optimum arousal. Recent neuroimaging evidence has found activation in the amygdala when extraverts see happy faces. Some researchers have also associated the presence of a specific gene (5HTT) with high neuroticism scores. We'll come back to some other neuroanatomical correlates of personality in chapter 9.

Eysenck's theory has been widely tested and most researchers agree that these traits are core human personality characteristics. However, the approach has been superseded by a more thorough model, the five-factor model or Big Five (which incorporates Eysenck's traits).

The Big Five

The current dominant model of personality is Macrae and Costa's Big Five, developed in the 1980s. The Big Five model proposes that we all differ along five personality dimensions – neuroticism, extraversion, openness, agreeableness, and conscientiousness – which can be measured using a questionnaire called the NEO-PI. The measure comprises simple statements such as 'I really like most people I meet', and people are asked to rate their accuracy on a five-point scale. There are also items that spouses and people who know a person well can answer, e.g. 'she has an active imagination'. The ratings of the respondent and the person who knows them tend to be very similar. There is also good evidence that these traits exists across cultures – although ratings vary between cultures (e.g. Americans and Europeans are more extravert but less agreeable than people from other cultures). People can also become acculturated – people who relocate from their country of origin become more like people in their adopted country in some ways (openness, but not introversion).

The trait approach is not without its critics, although the criticism is not as fierce now as it was in the 1970s when psychologists such as Walter Mischel argued that stable personality traits do not exist and that situations best predicted behaviour. The example of how we would behave at a party and a funeral appears to support this view (we would not start pulling party poppers at a funeral) although it is argued that in certain situations we can suppress or control the degree to which we exhibit our dominant personality traits and conform instead to social conventions.

Traits tend to be fairly stable across our life but there are some changes that occur. Extraversion, in particular, tends to be very stable. People tend to behave fairly consistently up until the age of thirty and stabilise between fifty and seventy. Conscientiousness and emotional stability increase between twenty and forty years but openness increases during adolescence and declines in old age. The way in which we view ourselves does change over time – research consistently shows that we rate our present selves far more positively than our past selves, supporting the well-known psychologist and country and western warbler, Mac Davis's, observation that 'Oh Lord, it's hard to be humble/When I'm perfect in every way/And I can't wait to look in the mirror/Because I get better looking each day.' In fact, research from the University of Cardiff shows that undergraduate women students, at least, feel they are more physically attractive towards the end of their course than the beginning. They also expect their future selves to be more attractive than their current selves.

We tend to rate ourselves as happier in the present than the past. However, very old people (over seventy) feel more positively about the present. Perhaps we feel more positive in the present for three reasons: (i) we cannot change the past,

(ii) we prefer to be seen in a favourable light in the present, or (iii) we can feel better about ourselves by denigrating the past.

Other personality tests

The Big Five is not the only personality test available, although it is one of the more valid and reliable. There is, for example, the Rorschach Inkblot test (first published in 1921) in which a person is asked what he or she sees in a card on which inkblots feature. This is an example of a projective test because people are thought to project their personalities onto the stimulus they respond to. The stimuli are ambiguous (e.g. an inkblot) and so responses might be revealing. Another projective test is the Thematic Apperception Test (developed in 1938) in which respondents are shown an ambiguous picture and asked what has happened, what will happen, what the characters are thinking, etc.

The problem with projective tests, however, is that they are almost universally invalid – some studies find no differences between the responses of the mentally ill and students. Reliability is worse – responses can change markedly from testing session to testing session. There are also no standardised procedures for administering these tests, so users can administer them in any way they see fit, which is not the ideal testing context.

The psychodynamic approach

The name, for better or worse, most closely associated with psychology is Sigmund Freud although, accurately, he should be most closely associated with psychoanalysis, a different beast altogether. Freud was a Viennese physician who, despite an early research career focusing on the neurobiological basis of mental disorder, made a significant impact on mental health and personality by studying patients who exhibited various behavioural problems, especially hysteria (where people feel paralysis of some part of the body despite there being no physiological basis for the condition).

One patient, in particular, provided the foundations for the entire Freudian theoretical edifice. Anna O. was seen by Freud and a fellow physician, Josef Breuer. She suffered from typical hysteria – loss of speech, limb paralysis, and so on, with no discernible organic cause. Under hypnosis it was discovered that the symptoms dated back to when she felt unable to express an emotion. When she experienced this emotion under hypnosis, the hysteria subsided (representing a catharsis). However, it was later discovered that she did not fully recover and took morphine for her symptoms, a fact of which Freud was apparently aware.

The case of Anna O. and others convinced Freud that human behaviour was motivated by instinctual drives (which could be triggered by traumatic events) that supplied 'psychic energy'. If this energy could not be discharged, behavioural disturbances followed. Traumatic events lead to the hiding of strong emotions, and the events and the emotions that generated the trauma are found in the unconscious. The unconscious exerts control over our observable behaviour. Unconscious traumatic events can also be prevented from reaching consciousness (a process called repression).

Because the recall of these events is only accessible during hypnosis (apparently), Freud argued that there were different levels of consciousness – the unconscious, conscious and preconscious (where events can be accessible to consciousness through effort). Freud also divided the mind into three structures:

- the *id*, which contains the libido (the primary source of instinctual drive), is completely unconscious and its aim is to obtain immediate gratification, a phenomenon called the pleasure principle.

- the *ego* is the self, controlling and integrating behaviour and mediating relations between the id and the superego and the demands of reality (and operates according to the reality principle).
- the *superego* is divided into the conscience and ego-ideal (the internalisation of a person's goals and aspirations) – it is the policeman of the unconscious.

Each of these structures is involved in conflict – the pressures of the reality and pleasure principles and the internalisation of goals see to that. The result is compromise formation – the superego and id reach a compromise, and this is revealed in dreams, slips of the tongue, and art.

Freud is probably best known for three aspects of his work: his book *The Interpretation of Dreams*, defence mechanisms, and his psychosexual theory of personality. According to Freud, dreams were the 'royal road' to the unconscious – they had manifest content (what the dream was superficially about) and a latent content (the hidden message, generated by the unconscious). Contents of the unconscious could also be indirectly accessed through free association – asking the person to clear their mind and report any thought or image that emerges.

When the id's drives come into conflict with the overbearing superego, and the person feels anxiety, the ego steps in with a series of defence mechanisms. The six most important defence mechanisms are:

- *repression* – keeping unpleasant thoughts out of conscious awareness.
- *reaction formation* – replacing a thought which provokes anxiety with one that doesn't (e.g. a person who watches pornography but whose superego does not allow its enjoyment becomes a rabid anti-pornography crusader).

- *projection* – a denial of unacceptable desires and finding them in the behaviour of others.
- *sublimation* – diverting energy from an unacceptable to an acceptable drive (e.g. sexual frustration may find an outlet in creating art).
- *rationalization* – inventing a rational explanation for a behaviour that is not acceptable.
- *conversion* – manifesting intrapsychic conflict through a physical symptom (as seen in Anna O.).

Freud's psychosexual theory argued that our personality developed by passing through various sexual stages in which we derived sexual pleasure from parts of the body (i.e. any gratification from the body, not necessarily orgasmic). If a person's development is arrested at one of these stages and cannot progress, he or she becomes fixated. Normal personality development involves passing through all stages, although Freud argued that most people become more or less fixated at a specific stage. The stages are:

- The oral stage – the child receives sexual gratification orally (sucking, biting, chewing, etc.). A person fixated at this stage may become very passive. Fixation later can lead to excessive talking, smoking and eating.
- The anal stage – at the age of two, infants begin to enjoy expelling faeces (expressive period) and, later, enjoy retaining them (retention period). A person fixated at the first period becomes destructive and cruel; at the second, miserly.
- The phallic stage – at age three, the infant derives pleasure from the penis or clitoris (Freud used the word phallus bisexually to mean penis or clitoris); he/she attaches itself to a parent of the opposite sex, noting sex roles of their parents. A boy's attachment to the mother is called the Oedipus

complex; a girl's to her father, the Electra complex. The boy may wish to take his father's place but fears his father will castrate or punish him. The boy changes when he begins to model his behaviour on his father; if he does not, he becomes preoccupied with demonstrating his masculinity.

- The latency period – occurs after the phallic stage and reflects a submerging of sexual drive until puberty at which point, the child enters:
- The genital stage – the sexual drive can find an outlet in heterosexual genital contact.

Freud's psychosexual theory is brilliant in its fantastical creativity and its persuasive plausibility. However, although children do become preoccupied by parts of their body and what they do at certain stages of development, there is little evidence linking this to later personality development.

After Freud: Jung, Adler, Horney and Erikson

Freud's work attracted many followers, some of whom did not agree completely with his outlook and developed variants of psychodynamic theory. Carl Jung, for example, was described by Freud as his 'crown prince and successor', but disagreed with the emphasis on sexuality and the structure of the unconscious. Psychodynamic theorists did not get on too well – when disagreements arose, they were like a sack of cats, an outcome which probably provided them with years of case material. Jung argued that we have a collective unconscious – memories and ideas inherited from our ancestors. Here, we store archetypes – inherited and universal thought patterns. Alfred Adler also minimised the importance of sexuality, emphasising instead the importance of inferiority. As infants, we rely on others for survival; as we develop we encounter and see others who are more gifted than us – intellectually, physically, athletically. Life, therefore, is a way of compensating for the deficits that we see in ourselves. To succeed, we engage in a striving for superiority, a major motivational force in life. Karen Horney also departed from the Freudian cause on sexuality, emphasising instead the anxieties that we have about relationships. To deal with the anxiety, we have three basic strategies: we can move towards others (accept the situation), move against them (resist and become aggressive), or move away (withdraw and become isolated). Erik Erikson emphasised the social aspects of personality development. He argued that personality develops across the lifespan (and is not determined primarily in child-hood) and through the crises that arise from social encounters with other people. People's personality, therefore, is constantly evolving – the term 'identity crisis' is Erikson's.

In evaluating psychodynamic theory, an immediate problem is testability. Many of the claims do not lend themselves to scientific testing and, therefore, cannot be rejected or accepted. Does the id exist? Does the ego? How do you demonstrate that the id's urges result in artistic creativity? Sometimes, the ideas actively work against science. If a person admits to unpleasant thoughts, that fits the theory; if he or she does not, they are repressing. An excellent dissection of psychodynamic theory can be found in Eysenck's *Decline and Fall of the Freudian Empire*.

7

The development of behaviour

The human infant is helpless. When it is born, it relies on its caregivers for nourishment, shelter, love, and education. Infants are not entirely without motivation, however, and there is evidence that they begin to interact with the environment quickly and their brains develop rapidly, with the evolutionarily oldest parts of the brain maturing first. As you saw in chapter 5, infants begin to speak by the age of two (the end of infancy). John Betjeman, in *Summoned by Bells*, noted that 'Childhood is measured out by sounds and smells/And sights before the dark of reason grows.' This chapter describes some of these perceptual and cognitive milestones.

Motor and perceptual development

Three of the infant's important movements are rooting, sucking, and swallowing, and all are reflexes (automatic). If you touch an infant's cheek it will turn towards the direction of the touch (this is called rooting); an object placed on the baby's lips will lead to sucking; when liquid enters its mouth, it makes automatic swallowing movements. With interaction with the environment, and maturation of its nervous system, the infant's movement becomes more exploratory, voluntary and sophisticated and interacts with its developing perceptual skills.

Movement is important to visual perception and much of

the infant and child's motor behaviour (orienting, sucking, moving the head or eyes) can tell us quite a lot about how it perceives the world, how it prefers certain stimuli over others and even what it remembers. For example, an infant will swallow tastes it likes and not those it dislikes (but is unable to tell you why because it cannot speak); it will move its head towards a cloth impregnated with a particular odour it was exposed to previously. We can measure an infant's eye movement precisely enough to investigate exactly what it scans and focuses on when it sees. For example, using this method, we know that one-month-olds tend not to examine the features of a stimulus but its contours (this is called the externality effect). This movement changes within a month or two and the eyes begin to look at stimulus features, presumably because the infant's acuity and its ability to distinguish different types of shade is developing. At three weeks, infants will prefer to look at checkerboards with large squares; by fourteen weeks, they prefer looking at small ones. At around three months, their ability to focus is comparable to adults' and, although they prefer to look at colours rather than greys when born, their ability to distinguish between colours is poor (this develops after two months).

The preference for looking at complex stimuli emerges gradually – infants begin to prefer looking at face-like stimuli and scrambled faces rather than a black-and-white oval. By two years of age, infants prefer natural face arrangements (rather than disorganised ones). There may be two explanations for this: the child may either compare stimuli for contrast and, if they are identical, analyse the structure; or the child has a mechanism for processing the structural aspects of people's faces (called conspec). Current research tends to support the latter rather than the former. Children (as well as adults) seem to recognise faces by examining the relations between the features in them, rather than focusing on specific features. There is also evidence that infants process faces whole; children with cataracts (but later treated) were better able to tell whether the tops or bottoms of people's faces in photographs matched compared with sighted children, suggesting that visual deprivation impairs the ability to process faces holistically.

Another important aspect of perceptual development is the appreciation of space: perceiving three-dimensional space and estimating distance (depth perception). This was famously demonstrated by the experiment involving a visual cliff. The visual cliff is a platform, part of which is solid and not transparent but continues as a solid, transparent shelf of glass. Underneath the glass part there is a checkerboard placed on the floor. In experiments by Gibson and Walk, six-month-old infants would crawl to the edge of glass but not go any further, as if they were afraid of falling (even though they would only be crawling on safe, solid glass). The babies had developed binocular depth perception – perceiving stimuli with both eyes – and this is a feature that is complete by around three years. Also rapidly developing are kinetic depth cues – by four weeks, infants will blink if they perceive an object looming towards them. This development is closely linked with motor development, because head movement helps the child navigate its way in the environment – babies with lots of crawling experience, for example, are more scared of the visual cliff.

Development of memory

What is the first memory you can remember? It's likely that it occurred after the age of four – we seem to exhibit what's called infantile amnesia for events before then although we can form memories of events at around thirteen months and three-year-olds can recall trips to a fast-food restaurant or what happened when they were two. Presumably, these are not transferred to long-term memory because we lack the language – as well as developed memory structures – to enable this to happen. To circumvent the problem of infants not being able to vocalise meaningfully, psychologists have devised other methods of measuring memory – for example, children will gaze longer at a stimulus they have seen before, or will re-enact a behaviour they see an adult do. In one study, around two-thirds of children who observed an adult switching on a light box imitated the adult; none of a control group did. The number of sequences of events an infant can remember increases from three at age twenty months, to five at twenty-four months, to eight at thirty months, suggesting that either memory capacity is expanding or their method of encoding is improving. Also, as infants grow older, the delay between encoding and retrieval increases: at fourteen months, for example, an infant can demonstrate the use of a prop one week after being exposed to it. One study read three stories to eight-month-old infants over ten days. Two weeks later, the infants listened longer to the words that appeared most frequently in the story than to those which did not.

At around three to four years, memory improves and the accuracy and amount of material recalled improves even more if the child is prompted by an adult. At around the age of two, children can imitate a series of actions they have seen adults perform, a week after seeing them. At the age of three, children begin imitating conversation and are better able to encode events verbally. Memory is also better if the child verbally describes the event at the time. Children also begin to introduce narrative into their recall (which improves retrieval), a process that happens at around four years.

The thinking child

The most comprehensive account of the development of cognition was presented by the Swiss psychologist, Jean Piaget.

Although it has its critics (and the criticisms, in many cases, are valid), the model of how the child begins to reason has had more influence on how psychologists view human cognitive development than any other. Piaget saw cognition as a maturational process – it goes through stages. He believed that children possessed cognitive structures, mental representations of rules for understanding the world, two of which are schemata (rules that define a particular type of behaviour, such as grasping) and concepts (rules describing properties of the environment, e.g. objects and what they do and what happens when they are manipulated). These develop via interaction with the world and two processes contribute to this – one where the child uses new information to make it fit with existing schemata (e.g. making an aeroplane noise while moving a washing up liquid bottle means the child has assimilated the bottle into the schema of a plane) and another where old schemata are changed by new experiences (e.g. discovering a new kind of animal and using the correct name for it, rather than using a name of another animal she knows). The processes are called assimilation and accommodation respectively.

According to Piaget, children pass through four stages of cognitive development:

1. Sensorimotor period (one to two years): the child begins to realise that objects do not disappear when out of sight (and will hunt for hidden objects); he/she begins to imitate the actions of others and show evidence of symbolic thinking (using words to represent objects).
2. The preoperational period (two to six/seven years): the ability to think symbolically and logically increases (a child will represent a train by using a series of blocks); language learning is rapid, but the concept of conservation is relatively poor – children will think there is more water in a tall, narrow container if they see it transferred from a stout, short

container; egocentrism increases – the child believes that everyone sees what he/she sees; e.g. a three-year-old playing hide and seek may run to a corner, turn his back and close his eyes thinking he cannot be seen; similarly, when asked to indicate what a doll might see from its perspective, the child attributes his own point of view to the object's.

3. The period of concrete operations (six/seven to eleven): the child can master conservation and can tell whether one concrete object is bigger/taller than another but is unable to do this abstractly.

4. The period of formal operations (eleven plus): children begin to reason in the abstract and can think hypothetically.

Piaget also emphasised the importance of play to development and thought of it as more than idling: it was cognitive activity. He called it symbolic play because an object could be used as another, different object (a pencil could be used to write and then used to mimic combing hair; a shoe box could be used as a doll's bath, and a blade of grass used as a thermometer to test the temperature of the imaginary water).

Challenges and alternatives to Piaget

While many of Piaget's observations have stimulated a mass of research and provided a framework which was once useful for studying cognitive development, modern research has questioned some of his conclusions. For example, the child's egocentrism is diminished when the agents whose point of view he/she is trying to adopt are made familiar or when the perspective-taking task is made easier. Also, three-year-old children know that when they look at a card and the person opposite is looking at the other side, they understand that the other person sees something different. Conservation may also be possible if

Piaget's tasks are simplified. For example, three- to five-year-old children who see sugar dissolved in water have been reported to say the sugar has not disappeared (as non-conservers would).

On a broader level, Piaget's research was not experimental (there was no control group and many studies consisted of observing his own children). Studies of the timetable for the four stages of development have failed to replicate this and children can be trained to perform a task they should only be capable of doing at another later stage. This last criticism suggests that the child has the ability but that the ability varies with age.

Piaget tended to discount experience in the development of his stages – when these stages occurred, they occurred (although studies suggest that some cultures not used to conservation do not develop this until age eleven). Lev Vygotsky, on the other hand, thought that culture and interaction with the social environment was critical to cognitive development. When the child hears others speak about the world and sees them react to it, this influences his/her thinking. A child not exposed to this stimulation would not develop adequately (as the extreme case of Genie showed in chapter 5). Vygotsky also argued that a child's speech influenced his/her development. Piaget argued that a child talking to itself would do so egocentrically and not communicatively (so that it would make sense to others) – it would be a me-me-me stream of consciousness; even children aged seven can be heard talking to themselves in this way. Vygotsky thought differently and suggested that this talk reflected plans that would guide later behaviour – children engage in more private speech when a task is hard (and those who do this are more attentive and better-performing). At around the age of seven, this external speech becomes 'inner speech', akin to that adults use when reading or solving a puzzle. Children's thinking also improves if they solve puzzles and problems with parents and teachers rather than with same-ability peers (a phenomenon Vygotsky grandly termed 'the zone of proximal or potential ability' – the range of skills the child cannot master without assistance). The support of carers provides cognitive scaffolding – a means of supporting learning, but a means that can be adjusted.

Emotional and social development

One of the most important determinants of a child's social development is attachment: the social and emotional bond between child and carer that ensures protection, comfort, and love. Some psychologists, such as John Bowlby, suggest that the need to bond is innate and that the child behaves in a way designed to elicit attachment behaviour from its parent – sucking, cuddling, looking, smiling, and crying – these behaviours, in themselves, serve physiological needs but they also encourage the adult to respond in a particular way. A baby monkey will cling onto the mother's chest after birth; this does not happen in humans but an infant will follow the contours of a carer's body when held.

Experiments by Harry Harlow in the 1970s emphasised how important comfort and feeling protected was to infants. Harlow found that when he separated baby monkeys from their mothers and raised them in a cage where the surrogate mother was made of bare wire which dispensed milk, or wire covered with padding and terry cloth but which did not dispense milk, the infants would prefer to cling and to hug the padded surrogate, only moving to the bare wire surrogate for food. Physical contact with soft material seems innately reinforcing (as we see when children cling onto security blankets).

Mothers find it extremely difficult not to smile at their babies and babies will respond to a mother's smile with a smile and will turn away, uninterested, if the mother does not respond. At around three months, a baby will respond to familiar faces but the type of smiling it engages in depends on the elicitor: cheek-raising is associated with responding to the mother's smiles, an open mouth with visual engagement with the mother. Crying is also an effective attachment behaviour – a mother will instinctively pick up and comfort a distressed child, thereby negatively reinforcing the crying.

Crying often occurs when the infant is in a strange environment, where the unfamiliarity provokes fear and distress. For example, between six and twelve months, infants will treat strangers warily or fearfully (this is called stranger anxiety), especially if the stranger is male (and less so if the stranger is another child). The anxiety is reduced if the mother is friendly towards the stranger. Fearful responses, clinging, and crying also occur when the child is separated from its mother (separation anxiety), and this can be seen between six and fifteen months.

This general anxiety may reveal more specific patterns of attachment. Margaret Ainsworth and her colleagues set up a series of experiments in which the infant and the carer were left in a strange room. The carer would leave and be reunited with the infant or a stranger would enter. On the basis of these experiments, Ainsworth described three types of attachment. Secure attachment arose when infants preferred mothers to strangers and would cry when its carer left the room. Resistant attachment arose when the infant approached and withdrew from the mother when she was reunited with the child; the child might continue crying or push her away. Finally, avoidant attachment arose when infants did not cry when the mother left and was indifferent when she returned. The last two types are very insecure forms of attachment.

Mothers who attend promptly to their child's distress have infants who are securely attached; indifferent mothers encourage avoidant attachment and mothers who are impatient with the child and are more interested in themselves foster resistant attachment. These forms of attachment have long-term effects.

Securely attached infants, for example, become sociable three-and-a-half-year-olds; insecurely attached infants have difficulty adjusting socially later in childhood, can be hostile, impulsive and withdrawn. (There are cross-cultural differences, however: German babies are more avoidant than American ones, perhaps because they are encouraged to be independent.) Maternal sensitivity is a significant predictor of secure attachment but the ability of the child and mother to synchronise behaviours, the presence of positive mood, and co-ordinated play are also important.

Sometimes, the child can show problems with emotional regulation. Depressed mothers, for example, express more negative emotion (not surprisingly) and engage less positively and responsively with their child. They can become hostile and rejecting so that the child forms greater attachment to a teacher or the father than the mother. This behaviour can have long-term effects on the child's adjustment – it has been associated with behavioural disturbances at home and with impaired play. There is also some EEG evidence to suggest that criers and non-criers have different patterns of brain activation – more right-sided activation is found in criers, consistent with a model of the brain and emotion described in chapter 9. Infants of depressed mothers show less left frontal activation (as do depressed mothers) than those of non-depressed mothers (but breast-feeding depressed mothers have children who show less right-sided activation). Sociable children have been found to show greater left frontal activation.

The mother's behaviour can also affect the first-born's behaviour when a new, second baby enters the family home. Mothers are less warm towards their older children when they give birth to a new baby, and children over two may feel less secure and become disruptive as a consequence. They may engage in competition with the newborn (sibling rivalry), although this depends on how secure the older child feels. Some families, however, only have one child – studies show that such children are high in self-esteem and motivation to succeed, are more obedient and are more intellectually able than children with siblings.

While attachment can determine a child's emotional and social outlook, there are some disorders seen in childhood that can seriously affect a child's social development. Autism, for example, which is characterised by social abnormality (such as inability to form social relations and interact spontaneously with others), language abnormality (delayed language development, idiosyncratic communication, neologisms and little social chat), and stereotypical and repetitive patterns of behaviour. The disorder was first described in 1943. There is a milder form called Asperger's Disease. Autistic individuals have difficulty in perceiving emotion in others – when sorting photographs into categories, autistic children would sort according to appearance (e.g. hat) rather than emotion, and autistic people cannot identify emotion in people's eyes (they also fail to maintain eye contact). Some autistic individuals, such as Kim Peek, the man who was inspiration for Dustin Hoffman's character in *Rain Man*, have exceptional skills such as the ability to memorise huge amounts of information (such as the works of Shakespeare) and recall this information months after encoding. He has learned 8000 books to date.

There is also evidence that people with autism are unable to infer the mental states of others, i.e. they lack a theory of mind. This is easily tested in the laboratory by using a 'false-belief task'. Here, Person A places an object in a cupboard and leaves the room. Person B enters, puts the object in a different location and leaves. Person A re-enters and the participant is asked where Person A will look for the object. Children of five or six years answer this correctly – Person A will look in the cupboard. Younger children give the wrong answer – Person A would look in the place where Person B put it. Deaf children perform worse than hearing children on this test, with older deaf children performing better than younger deaf children. In autism, Simon Baron-Cohen termed this inability to infer another's thoughts as 'mindblindness'. Others have suggested that autistic children have difficulty seeing objects as wholes, attending to detail where most of us would process situations and objects more globally.

Pink for girls? The development of sex roles

In a very revealing experiment carried out by a group of US researchers, the permission of parents visiting a Californian museum was sought to film and record their interactions with their children as they made their way around the exhibitions. Data were collected from 298 interactions between mothers and fathers and their daughters and sons on twenty-six days over a thirty-month period. Conversations were rated according to whether they involved explanations, descriptions of, or directions for, exhibitions. The researchers found that parents were more likely to explain exhibits to their sons than to their daughters, thus implicitly suggesting that the boys would be more interested in science than would the girls.

Parents play an important part in shaping their children's sex roles – cultural norms regarding how each sex should behave. Thus, boys are rewarded for playing with footballs, toy guns, cars, and trucks; girls are rewarded for playing with dolls, tea sets, and make-up. Interestingly, parents tend to encourage baby boys to increase their motor activity whereas they are more soothing with girls.

In terms of how the child begins to recognise him/herself as a boy or a girl and follows the stereotypes that go along with these, one theorist suggests that it proceeds through three stages.

At the first, when the child is about two to three years, the child learns the label that people have given him/her (boy/girl) and adopts this as part of his/her identity. At the second stage, between three and four years, the child recognises similar characteristics of his/her sex in others and can tell the difference between boys and girls. At the third stage, the child learns that their and others' sex is constant – if they dress up as a boy/girl, they are still a girl or boy, respectively. The child is argued to have a mental representation of what each sex 'means' and uses information it receives to develop this representation. By the age of two, children seem to prefer to play with others of their own sex: this preference increases exponentially as the child develops. By two, they will also spontaneously play with sex-typical toys but while most children can discriminate between girls' and boys' toys, they are not as good at discriminating between sex-typed activities such as drawing, playing with dolls, making cake vs. climbing, chasing, playing cowboys. In one study of two-year-olds, only one child in eight could.

Stereotypes can be distorting. In one study, a six-month-old baby was dressed in pink or blue and parents were asked to give it either a doll, a train, or a toy fish. The baby in pink would be given the doll more often than would the baby in blue. Parents also smiled more at the pink-clad infant.

Sex differences emerge significantly after puberty, and not only at the obvious physical level. Girls worry about their weight and the size of their hips and breasts; boys worry about their height, their musculature, and size of their genitals. Even eight- to eleven-year-old children are now concerned with muscle development. By the age of fifteen, girls become very dissatisfied with their bodies (partly through discussing this with peers and comparing themselves to desirable others) and depression is greater in adolescent girls than boys: a study from the MRC Social and Public Health Sciences Unit at Glasgow in 2003 found that psychological distress is increasing significantly in girls.

Boys see adolescence as a time of freedom; girls see their behaviour as being more restricted. This time also sees the testing of boundaries, norm-breaking, conflict with parents and exploring new things (and often things adolescents should keep well away from). Early-maturing girls are more likely to drink, smoke, and date (and have older friends). Very early and very late maturing boys, according to one study from the University of Edinburgh, are more likely to be rebellious (being sent out of class, swearing, being expelled). Early maturing boys drink because that's what their peers do, late maturers because it is a means of gaining popularity. Most adolescents, however, feel happy and self-confident.

Moral reasoning

Take a look at this vignette:

> A woman is near death from cancer. One drug might save her, a form of radium discovered by a chemist living in the same town, who is selling the drug at ten times what it cost him to manufacture it. The sick woman's husband tried to borrow the money but could raise only half the price. He told the chemist that his wife was dying and asked him to sell the drug more cheaply or, at least, let him pay later, but the chemist refused. The desperate husband broke into the chemist's shop to steal the drug for his wife. Should he have done that?

This was one of the moral dilemmas posed by Lawrence Kohlberg to a group of ten- to seventeen-year-old boys. On the basis of the responses he received, he proposed that children's moral reasoning develops through three levels. At the first level, children blindly obey authority and avoid punishment (preconventional level). In the vignette above, they would fear the man being punished for letting his wife die. This progresses to a later, more hedonistic evaluation – are the consequences pleasant or unpleasant? At the next level, children want to be regarded as good and realise that there are social norms that dictate behaviour (conventional level). In the example, the man should steal the drug or people would think him heartless. This thinking then progresses to moral rules and laws being seen as instruments to maintain social order. At the final level, people realise that moral rules are underpinned by principles (postconventional level); they realise that rules are social contracts, that people in authority are fallible and individual rights can sometimes supersede law. They learn to adopt ethical principles that are universal. According to Kohlberg, not all of us reach the postconventional level.

However, some have challenged Kohlberg's model. Boys exclusively, for example, were used as the basis of the model. When men and women are given the above dilemma, women operate at the second level; men at the third. Also, simple changes to the wording of the dilemma – such as emphasising the likelihood of imprisonment – leads to more preconventional levels of reasoning. There are also some cultural differences – one study found that Americans thought that the man should steal the drug, because the wife should live, but the Japanese though he shouldn't because they were concerned with the purity of life.

There are alternatives to this model. One is based on the concept of distributive justice. Here, the child makes moral decisions that are egocentric to begin with and makes decisions based on his/her own feelings and perspectives. This thinking then progresses to notions of equality – everybody should share in a reward, for example. The next stage sees equality giving way to concepts of merit and reciprocity and distribution of resources based on achievement. At the fourth and final stage (at around age ten/eleven), the child makes reasoning decisions based on the concept of fairness. There is some evidence to support this model. Some, however, have questioned whether 'moral development' is a valid descriptor, preferring instead to distinguish between 'moral' reasoning (where the consequences could be psychologically or physically harmful) and 'socio-conventional' reasoning (where decisions are informed by social norms, e.g. not dribbling while people are eating at a dinner table).

Of course, moral decisions are also emotional decisions and have emotional consequences (and emotional antecedents). In chapter 9, we'll explore the nature of emotion in more detail. We'll also examine the role of emotion in health and ill-health. The final chapter takes this theme a step further when we consider the nature of mental illness, its causes, and its treatment.

8

Influencing others: social psychology in action

Social cognition

You're about to go on a date with a friend of a friend of yours. You've not met him (or her) before and your friend gives you a brief personality sketch of your potential beau (or belle). He or she is intelligent, witty, industrious, polite, cold, and well-spoken. How well do you think your evening went? Well, barring a catastrophe, probably quite well but it might have gone better. Why? The word 'cold'.

Research carried out by Solomon Asch in the 1940s found that when people rated a hypothetical person described in a similar way, replacing the word 'cold' with 'warm' led people to judge the hypothetical person as happier, more generous, and altruistic. The effect extended to real life. Students told that their lecturer was 'cold' rated him as much more unsociable, self-centred, irritable, humourless, and ruthless than one described as 'warm'. This is an example of impression formation and we are susceptible to these influences all of the time. Note how politicians or their apparatchiks, for example, manipulate the media by making *ad hominem*, irrational, irrelevant remarks about opponents.

Asch also found a primacy effect for such descriptions. For example, people who were asked to judge hypothetical others described as:

intelligent, industrious, impulsive, critical, stubborn, and envious evaluated them more favourably than if they were described as:

envious, stubborn, critical, impulsive, industrious, and intelligent

The only difference between these lists is the word order.

Impression formation, as this is called, is only one type of behaviour studied by social psychologists. Gordon Allport defined social psychology as the study of 'how the thoughts, feelings and behaviour of individuals are influenced by the actual, imagined or implied presence of others'. Impression formation is an aspect of social cognition – what we think about ourselves and others – and we form impressions based not just on hearsay (as in Asch's example above) but appearance, dress, hairstyle, physical attractiveness, expertise, politics, accent, articulacy, age, and many, many other factors.

Others' impressions of us, and what we are told about ourselves, are not just trivial; they can be harmful. Experiments have shown that when women (and people from different races) are told that their specific group is generally poor at some cognitive task, they end up performing more poorly than those not told this. Now, imagine the same scenario played out to a child who is told she is useless and will not amount to anything. It takes some resilience, a thick skin, and tremendous self-esteem (or complete lack of self-awareness) to obviate the effects of others' opinions of us. We are disproportionately influenced by negative information about people – and bad impressions are very difficult to shift, probably because negative information signifies potential harm or danger.

The information we hold about people is stored as schemata – mental representations of others (they are very similar to stereotypes when applied to groups). We have them for friends, groups of people (e.g. vicars, bailiffs), and events (how to behave at a funeral). You probably have schemata regarding academics and psychologists. I remember attending one job interview, just as I was writing up my PhD. I was irked by questions from a panel member whom I mistook for a student representative – he had a shock of orange spiky hair and was dressed in a silver jumpsuit. I later discovered he was one of the country's best known psychologists. My schemata of what an academic should be, and the way for an interview panel to dress, did not extend to having hair like an exploding armchair, and astronaut couture. (I didn't get the job.)

Stereotypes are a psychological shorthand, summarising a group in a few traits, and some of these are harmless – Brits have stiff upper-lips, Germans are not famed for their sense of humour, and Italians (well, Italian men) pinch ladies' bottoms. We learn these through socialisation, rather than through direct experience, and stereotypes influence our interaction with the stereotyped person – if we are told someone (or a group) is lazy, we will treat them accordingly. They, in turn, may conform to the stereotype because this is what is expected of them. There are also pernicious stereotypes. A study from the US which analysed the facial features of prison inmates at the Florida Department of Corrections, and correlated these with sentence harshness, found that prisoners with Afro-centric features received harsher sentences.

Sometimes, our stereotypes and our prejudices can be revealed indirectly using a measure called the implicit association test (see http://implicit.harvard.edu/implicit to try this test for yourself). In this test, your reaction is measured to how appropriate you think word pairs are. So, in experiments testing biases towards the obese, people tend to respond more quickly to the word pairing 'thin people–good' and 'fat people–bad' than 'thin people–bad', 'fat people–good'. It reveals the stereotype and implicit bias we have against fat people because explicitly we say we are not prejudiced.

Making inferences about others

Before looking at how we judge others, it's useful to briefly note how we see ourselves. We tend to be very self-aware but some social psychologists suggest we have two selves – the private self (our own thoughts and feelings) and public self (the self we like to portray, the one that creates a good impression). Reduced self-awareness leads to deindividuation (and a person can be uninhibited and impulsive); at the extreme, such deindividuation can result in riots and the disregard and violation of the dignity of human beings (as evidenced at Abu Ghraib prison). If our actual self is not matched by our public self, we can feel sad and dejected. If the public persona does not match the personal self, we can feel anxious or afraid.

A favourite word in the social cognitivist's vocabulary is 'attribution'. All of us are social psychologists, in our way (the novelist Malcolm Bradbury once wrote that a sociologist can do anything and call it work; this can probably be extended to social psychologists). We have ideas of why people behave in the way they do and that their behaviour is predictable (so, if we are kind to people, they are more likely to like us and return the favour). The common-sense understanding of what causes others' behaviour is explained by attribution theory. In fact, there is more than one theory but we'll focus on the most popular here.

We think that people behave in the way they do because environmental conditions make them do so (situational factors) or because their personality makes them so (dispositional factors). According to one variant of attribution theory, we attribute external (situational) or internal (dispositional) causes to people's behaviour by considering three things: consensus, consistency, and distinctiveness of behaviour. Consensual behaviour is behaviour we would expect of most people – someone who lends a person a coin to make a phone call may not be regarded as generous because that is what most people would do (external). If they refused to lend a coin, however, they would be regarded as miserly (internal). We also judge people according to how consistently they behave. If they behave consistently (effervescent all of the time), we attribute the behaviour to internal causes (they are bubbly people); if inconsistently, we attribute external causes (only bubbly in response to certain events). Finally, we note how often a person behaves in a specific way only in specific situations – a child who is obnoxious only in the company of his friend would lead you to suggest that the friend is a bad influence on the child (external cause); a child who is obnoxious to everyone might be regarded as generally obnoxious (internal cause).

As you saw in the section on reasoning errors in chapter 6, we seem to be methodical and scientific in our analyses of people's behaviour but commit errors of judgement. One of these is called the fundamental attribution error. When we see a car driver make a mistake, we tend to think that he/she is incompetent, rather than thinking that he/she has been deflected by his/her child screaming in the back seat, or has heard an alarmingly ominous noise coming from the engine, or has had to avoid another driver. We tend to attribute other people's behaviour to dispositional factors – and this is the fundamental attribution error. This was famously illustrated in an experiment in the 1960s when participants were asked to judge the attitude of students writing pro- or anti- essays about Castro. When participants were told that the writers had been free to write what they wanted, they inferred that the pro-Castro writers were genuinely pro. However, when it was made clear to the participants that writers had been told what position to take, they still inferred that the writers believed what they had written (the right, situational reasons for writing were disregarded).

But as humans, we can be contrary. When judging our own behaviour, we are more likely to attribute it to situational factors – our behaviour is variable, but others' is fairly stable (this is called the actor–observer effect). This was brilliantly illustrated by a study in which student couples were asked to explain their attributions for arguments they had. When commenting on their own behaviour, people would attribute arguments to situational factors (e.g. financial difficulties, lots of university work); when referring to their partner, the behaviour was attributed to their personality (they were selfish, lacked commitment, etc.). Two reasons for the error may be that our focus of attention is different for ourselves and others. When someone else behaves, the focus is on their salient behaviour rather than the situation they are in. Alternatively, we know ourselves well, that our behaviour can be variable and that it can be influenced by situations.

Another error is false consensus – people believe that their view is widely shared and is the norm, possibly because they surround themselves with similar others or only look for supporting, rather than disqualifying, evidence in their environment. We also tend to attribute our great successes to internal causes and our failures to external causes (this is called the self-serving bias). So, poor performance on a test is attributed to a hard or unfair set of questions, rather than lack of understanding, knowledge or preparation. The error probably occurs because it is a means of protecting self-esteem. This becomes especially important in mental illnesses such as depression. Here, people with a depressive attributional style will attribute failure to stable and global causes such as lack of ability, rather than bad luck or some other external cause. A related error is the belief that, in a just world, people get what they deserve. People attribute others' misfortune to the person rather than the situation – at the extremes, the unemployed, those who have been raped, those with HIV, and those who have suffered genocide are all to blame for their misfortune. People who commit this type of error tend to be wealthy and have high social status.

Attitudes

An ex-chief constable extols the efficiency of security windows; an elderly actress eulogises a stairlift; a rich comedian pretends to work in a supermarket's in-store bakery and offers unsuspecting customers a loaf; important-looking men and women in white coats in white laboratories try to sell you white paste in a white tube to whiten your not-so-white teeth. All of these people are trying to do something (apart from create annoyance): they want us to have a positive attitude towards the product they are promoting, and if their expert and appealing persona is convincing, we should be even more enamoured of the product because these people are trustworthy. Some of them even wear white coats.

Our attitudes – a relatively enduring set of beliefs and intentions regarding people, events, and ideas – govern much of our social behaviour and they can be swayed relatively easily (we may even rationalise why we hold two contradictory attitudes). Sometimes, even being exposed to the same stimulus over and over again can change our attitude of it – one study found that people liked nonsense words more, the more often they saw them, even when the stimuli were barely visible (this is called the mere exposure effect). Our attitudes are sometimes completely at odds with our behaviour – a study in the 1930s had a researcher driving across the USA with a Chinese couple, stopping off at hotels and restaurants. Only one in 250 refused to serve the couple. When the businesses were later asked whether they would have served the Chinese couple, ninety-two per cent said they wouldn't, a general finding reflected in other research showing that attitudes are poor predictors of actual behaviour. A currently popular model of explaining the relationships between the two is the theory of reasoned action and planned behaviour. This argues that a person's intention to behave is predicted by whether they like that behaviour, their perception of the number of other people who also like that behaviour, by having the resources to engage in it, and the behaviour is very specific. Using this model, one study accurately predicted which of 600 UK drivers assessed would engage in idiotic driving.

Our attitudes can be changed by the source of the information we strike an attitude about, the message itself and the type of people we are. For example, as the opening to this section suggests, the credibility and attractiveness of the source is important. People are more likely to believe information about preventative medicine if it is published in a medical journal than in *Pravda* or a mass circulation tabloid. People who believed that eight hours' sleep was good for them changed their attitude when told that a Nobel prize-winning sleep researcher recommended less sleep. Attractive people are also more likely to persuade us to do things such as sign a petition. People who are similar to us are more likely to persuade us in matters of taste, but dissimilar people are more likely to persuade us on matters of fact. People with very low or very high self-esteem are less likely to be persuaded than are those with average self-esteem but men and women seem to be equally persuadable. One model of persuasion suggests that we change attitudes based on thinking substantially about an argument's strengths and weaknesses and whether the persuasion is positive and has emotional appeal (hence, the use of celebrities in adverts).

However, not all of us will be rushing to the telephone to order a stairlift or security window, while thinking of popping down to the shop for a baguette and some toothpaste. Most attempts at persuasion fail, and for good reason. We have a tendency to resist persuasion, especially if it is obvious (a process called reactance). If we are forewarned that we are about to be persuaded, we become more resistant to it. We can also be inoculated – a weak argument is put forward and this builds up resistance, via counter-arguments.

Of course, we can sometimes feel a little anxious if we hold two contrary attitudes or if our behaviour is not consistent with our attitudes, a phenomenon known as cognitive dissonance. For example, if you think you are really good at your job, but you fail to get a pay increment year on year, the gulf between your attitude and expectation causes dissonance. To reduce this, you might think that the money isn't that important, or that the company is being stupidly harsh, undervalues real achievement or cannot afford the increases, or you can reassess your view: you either work better or revise your opinion of your work. All of us experience this sort of dissonance – we all probably have friends, for example, whose religious, political or ethical views are contrary to ours yet they still remain as friends. The rogue trader justifies selling shoddy goods because it earns him a good living and 'doesn't do anyone any harm'. Dissonance also explains another social phenomenon – the fact that we value an item more if it costs more. This, at least, applies to expensive items such as designer clothes and perfume (even though cheaper items use the same materials). We also rate things we have to fight or work hard for more highly than those we didn't (even if the work or the fight has been unpleasant, or imposed on us).

Influencing others

We saw in the last section that one way of changing a person's attitude is to influence them and two processes important for social influence are compliance, where we behave in a way which does not change our underlying belief, and conformity, where we behave in a way where our belief is changed. So, how can you get people to do what you would like them to do?

Psychologists have identified at least three techniques: ingratiation, reciprocity, and multiple requests. Getting people to like you will obviously make them more likely to do what you ask – and the more attractive the message-giver the better. A study in the 1960s found that a car was judged to go faster, to be better designed and more expensive if people saw an advert with an attractive woman next to the car than when not. Getting others to return a favour is also an important influence – if someone invites us for dinner, we like to reciprocate; if a company gives us a gift, we feel obliged to hear what its representative has to say. A random act of kindness is also reciprocated – one study found that when participants in an experiment were given a soft drink from a fellow participant, they bought more raffle tickets from the drink-giver when later asked. Finally, we can make multiple requests – starting small and leading up to big (the first part is called foot-in-the-door; the second, door-in-the-face). A series of small steps is usually better to get people to do what you would like – if the first few are successful, people have committed to a course of action.

Commitment is important – one study of energy consumption (actually, a psychology experiment) told half of those participating in an energy saving scheme that their involvement would be celebrated by being publicised in the local newspapers. The other half was not. When gas consumption was measured, those who had given public commitment consumed less gas than did those who gave a private commitment. The door-in-the-face approach is much bolder. One study asked participants if they would act as volunteers in a youth offenders' centre for a few weeks. None did. However, when they were then given a more dilute request – would they help take some offenders around a zoo for a couple of hours? – around half of the group agreed, presumably because they felt that a concession had been made. Both requests need to come from the same person to be effective. This has an echo in the louche English historian and politician Alan Clark's philosophy of life – always suggest the most extreme example because people will be more easily persuaded by your next, less extreme suggestion. Another technique involves getting a commitment and then changing the rules – for example, if you agreed to turn up for a meeting, but were then told that it would be at 7am, you would be more likely to agree to this than if you were told straight away that it was at 7am.

Some influences, however, are not subtle. They are commands and diktats and orders and we are surprisingly susceptible to following them. One author cites a patient who was given a prescription for ear drops which read 'place in R ear'; the patient misread this as 'rear'. Why he would think ear drops would go in his rear is a mystery but it illustrates the hold authority has over us – if the doctor said rear, it must be right (so to speak). Even the most powerful man in the world complies. At a United Nations meeting on 14 September 2005, George W. Bush was photographed writing a note to his aide: 'I think I need a bathroom break? Is this poss?'

Perhaps the classic, most famous – infamous – demonstration of this is Stanley Milgram's series of experiments on obedience to authority. Milgram recruited participants by placing adverts for a learning experiment in the local newspaper. In the experiment, the experimenter's stooge (a middle-aged accountant) was strapped to a chair (to prevent excessive movement when he was 'shocked') and electrodes were placed on his wrists. Participants were taken to another room, away from the stooge, where a device with dials and buttons awaited them. Participants were told that they would deliver an electric shock to the stooge whenever he gave a wrong answer in the (sham) learning experiment. The switches delivered shocks of between 15 and 450 volts (or so the participants thought). The volts would increase by 15 every time. Although the shocks were 'extremely painful', participants were told that 'they cause no permanent damage'. Under the switches were the legends 'Slight shock' to 'Danger: severe shock'.

When the learner made a mistake, the experimenter would order the participant to deliver the shock. At 300 volts, the learner was heard pounding on the wall and then said/did nothing. As no answer was considered incorrect, a shock would be ordered and the learner would pound the wall again. If the participant hesitated, the experimenter would say 'please go on' or, with further hesitation, 'The experiment requires you continue' or 'You have no other choice; you must continue'. What maximum voltage do you think most participants delivered? Most delivered 450 volts, despite all of the wall-pounding. When confederate and participant were in the same room, around a third obeyed the order to shock. A third were even willing to hold the stooge's hand as they delivered the shock.

The experiments showed that ordinary people can blindly follow orders. Other studies have shown that the uniform participants wear can also dictate the strength of punishment delivered. In one study, people dressed as nurses gave fewer shocks than did those dressed like the Ku Klux Klan (who delivered the most). As Stuart Sutherland wrote in his book, *Irrationality*, 'If uniforms have such strong effects in an experiment, how much more powerful is their influence likely to be on those genuinely entitled to wear them.' The echoes of Nazism are not far away.

Milgram found that one way of reducing slavish obedience was to have a stooge who was non-compliant – if the stooge did not comply, the number of shocks dropped. Despite the extreme nature of the experiment, and what you might think was the psychologically disturbing nature of their actions, eighty-four per cent of participants were glad they had participated (and none required psychiatric help).

In Milgram's experiment, participants complied. However, when we conform, the group around us establishes the social norm and we conform to that norm. This was well demonstrated in a brilliant series of experiments by Solomon Asch. He asked groups of seven to nine students to estimate orally the length of lines they saw on a screen: the target line was on the left and three alternatives appeared on the right. In fact, only one of the participants was genuine – the rest were stooges and on twelve of the eighteen trials gave the wrong answer. When this happened, seventy-five per cent of the genuine participants agreed: they went along with the decision even though it looked wrong but thought there might be something awry with their sight or that they had misunderstood the instructions. Those who didn't conform felt uncomfortable. When at least one other person dissented, however, the conformity dropped substantially. The dissent need not have been correct – those giving even more extreme wrong answers reduced conformity. People like to think their attitudes are right and when so many people disagree with them, they might change these attitudes; people also like to be liked and so by expressing disagreement they jeopardise this need. They also may feel as if they belong to a group (and share group identity) and, therefore, conform to the group.

People in groups

Eliot Aronson, the great American social psychologist, called one of his most entertaining books, *The Social Animal*. As humans, we enjoy the company of others. In fact, we cannot succeed or live effectively if we do not have contact with others. Being in a group gives us a sense of identity, gives us comfort and a sense of security. Being excluded from a group – being ostracised – can be psychologically damaging and reduce self-esteem. The feeling of belonging is so strong that a deviant member of an in-group can be treated more harshly than an equally deviant member of a group to which we do not belong (the outgroup). This is called the black-sheep effect.

Experiments have shown that the presence of others can make us work harder and more efficiently if the task is relatively simple (a phenomenon called social facilitation). The psychologist Zajonc (pronounced zai-on-ss) suggested that this was because others increase our level of arousal or drive. When people engage in difficult tasks, the arousal often impairs our performance – people who find mental arithmetic or spelling challenging, for example, find them almost impossible in the presence of others. An alternative view suggests that others make us self-aware and we try to make our actual self consistent with our ideal self. Another suggests that the presence of other stimuli is distracting – noise, for example, increases performance on simple tasks but impairs it on difficult tasks.

Sometimes, being a member of a group makes us a little indolent – little effort is made (this is called social loafing). A study from 1913 showed that people engaged in a tug-of-war game exerted less effort as a group than they would have individually. The ability to be identified obviously reduces loafing – an experiment in which people were asked to shout as loudly as they could, but one group was told that the group's volume would be measured whereas another was told that individual voices would be recorded, found that the former group shouted less loudly. Women are also less susceptible to loafing, as are people from Eastern cultures (compared with Western ones). Of course, if the task is made attractive and there is an element of competition with an out-group, social loafing is reduced. Studies also show that people will loaf more if the decisions the group makes are trivial or inconsistent with their own beliefs. So, the key to group work is to keep the group small, keep the topic relevant, meaningful and important and have an aim that has important consequences.

Research shows that group decisions follow certain rules: for example, they tend towards unanimity – opposing, extreme or novel views are sidelined so conformity is encouraged; they normally bow to the majority; a two-thirds majority is needed to establish a decision; and the first-shift phenomenon prevails – the group will make a decision consistent with the first shift in opinion put to it.

A direct way of encouraging group collaboration is brainstorming, where people uninhibitedly generate as many creative ideas as possible. Research shows that brainstorming reduces creativity and productivity but it can work if the process is done via email or if the group is heterogeneous.

There are well-documented flaws in group decision-making. Decisions made by groups tend to be more extreme and risky if the group tends towards risk (conversely, if the group tends towards caution, the decision will be very cautious). There is also the danger of groupthink – the tendency to avoid dissent and reach a consensus. The phrase was used by a psychologist to describe the fiasco that was Robert Kennedy's decision to overturn the Castro regime in Cuba by invading the Bay of Pigs. One of Kennedy's advisors, Arthur Schlesinger, advised against the invasion but was told : 'the President has made his mind up. Now is the time for everyone to help him all they can'. Some presidents, however, are surprisingly perceptive about yes-men: Ronald Reagan wrote:

> In any top position, you risk becoming isolated. People tell you about what you want to hear and are reluctant to tell you about somebody who might not be pulling his weight or doing something hurtful to your administration. Not many people close to you are willing to say: 'You're wrong'.

People will go with the flow to avoid upsetting the apple cart, or to avoid being sacked or ridiculed, or to avoid being seen as awkward or a trouble-maker. Groupthink is more likely if (i) the group is cohesive, (ii) its members think alike, balk at criticism and are unwilling to countenance alternative ideas/courses of action/an argument's strengths and weaknesses, (iii) the situation is stressful, and (iv) its leader has a dominant, clear point of view. To avoid the bad decisions arising from groupthink, therefore, criticism should be encouraged, an alternative view from outside the group should be introduced, and the group should be fractured.

Two's company ...

People behave differently in crowds (more differently even than in groups, which tend to be smaller). Crowds tend to occur at public events – football matches, pop concerts, demonstrations, funerals of members of the royal family, and so on. Sometimes, they get ugly and violence spills around them. Some theorists suggest that this is due to deindividuation – the loss of sense of identity – or the propulsion of group identity where people with common interests come together to achieve a shared goal. The psychologist Phillip Zimbardo found that women were likely to be twice as aggressive if their identity was concealed (they wore hoods and no name tags) than if it was overt. The degree of crowd activity will depend on local conditions – studies of the 1998 World Cup, for example, showed that the more heavy-handed the policing, the greater the violence from the supporters. Zimbardo was also the psychologist who created the now infamous Stanford Prison experiment. To examine the nature of conformity and deindividuation, Zimbardo took healthy, intelligent young men and randomly assigned them to the role of guard or prisoner in a mocked-up prison in the basement of Stanford University. In Zimbardo's words, this is what happened:

> At the end of only six days, we had to close down our mock prison because what we saw was frightening. It was no longer apparent to us or most of the subjects where they ended and their roles began ... In less than a week, the experience of imprisonment undid (temporarily) a lifetime of learning ... We

were horrified because we saw some boys (guards) treat other boys as if they were despicable animals, taking pleasure in cruelty, while other boys (prisoners) became servile, dehumanized robots who thought only of escape.

Prejudice

The difference between the police and the hooligans in the last section illustrates an inter-group problem, and inter-group behaviour tends to be competitive and 'ethnocentric' – one group will regard their own values as being superior to those of the other group. A series of studies with eleven-year-olds at a US summer camp in the 1950s illustrated this perfectly. The boys were split into two groups and each developed its own identity; they took part in competitions which became increasingly heated – taunts and insults led to one team ransacking the other's cabin. They developed genuine hatred for each other. The experimenters then orchestrated a serious problem – the water supply was sabotaged – and both groups had to co-operate to solve it. When this occurred, the conflict diminished. The psychologist behind the study, Musar Sherif, argued that when groups have mutually exclusive goals, they will compete with each other and this competition fosters mutual dislike. When the groups have a common goal, the co-operation reduces hostility.

When one or other group's goal is frustrated, the tendency to aggress increases. They feel angry and an outlet for the aggression needs to be found (this is called the frustration-aggression hypothesis). A group can feel deprived, relative to another group, and this causes aggression (this may explain conflicts from revolutions to racist violence in communities where the 'indigenous' group feels hard done by). The deprivation can also be experienced at the individual level – where a person compares his or her own status with another who appears to be preferentially treated – which can lead to depression and anger.

When the anger is generated by a negative view of a member of an outgroup simply on the basis that the member belongs to that outgroup, you have prejudice. When the view translates into behaviour, it becomes discrimination. We can develop prejudice about almost any group we tend not to identify with, which may compete with us and which we do not respect. The most common sources, however, tend to be race, sex, disability, mental health, nationality, religion, sexual orientation, and age. Membership of the group activates a schemata of that group so that the member is viewed stereotypically and becomes stigmatised. The stigmatised member can, in turn, develop attributional ambiguity interpreting any – innocuous – behaviour in others as prejudicial or discriminatory, even positive behaviour – 'Did I get the job just because I was black/a woman/in a wheelchair, etc.', they might ask.

One historical reason for prejudice suggested that the prejudiced people had authoritarian personalities – extremely disciplined children idealised their parents and all authority figures, and this extended into adulthood where weakness was belittled. A more recent model suggests that prejudiced individuals have a desire for their own group to be dominant, and reject egalitarian philosophies. Either way, prejudice tends to form in groups which perceive injustices between their and another group's status, which leads to hatred and conflict. The perceived injustices may be illusory – an act committed by a minority group, for example, is extended to represent the whole group's general behaviour even though there is no evidence that such a correlation actually exists. Recent research suggests that people tend to talk about negatively perceived outgroups in more abstract, general terms whereas they talk about the ingroup in more positive but concrete, descriptive language.

How can prejudice be reduced? Propaganda, government

schemes, and education have little effect – they reflect societal expectations but the ingroup attitudes are too well entrenched to accept these. Suppressing the stereotype is also ineffective – this simply makes the stereotype stronger. One way of reducing this bias is to get people thinking about their stereotype. One study of children who were asked to think what life must be like for a blind or disabled child, were more likely to go on a picnic with them than those who were not.

Does direct contact work? Not entirely. It does foster inter-racial interaction and some relationships are formed, but contact with an outgroup does not necessarily change racial stereotypes. Often, the stereotypes are confirmed. If a member of an ingroup has successful relations with a member of an outgroup, this can lead other members to view the outgroup more positively because this begins a sharing of information and a breakdown of unjustified stereotypes.

Love and hate

In 1997, 866 Americans were murdered at work, principally by customers; eighty per cent of non-fatal assaults in one study of eight Californian cities were due to angry and disgruntled clients. There are many places you expect aggression but, unless you're a boxer, in the army or the emergency services, the workplace isn't one of them. Human aggression is probably an evolutionary hangover from a time when the ability to hurt was necessary for our ability to survive and fight off attack. Most of our aggression is intraspecific (one species attacks its own members) and we are adept at both producing threat gestures to communicate an intent to aggress if provoked – we will stretch to our full height, maintain total eye contact, and close the space between us and our intended victim – as well as producing appeasement gestures, which are designed to avoid aggression.

Often, both gestures are ritualised and do not lead to actual conflict (which is adaptive) but serve to make clear to a competitor that they should stay clear.

Human aggression can occur in extreme forms (such as murder) to more subtle forms (as seen in bullying at school and the workplace). Some researchers have suggested that there are three categories of aggression: competitive and socially sanctioned (as seen in sport); premeditated (as seen in the armed forces, police, and criminals); and, the most common, impulsive. Usually facilitated by alcohol and drugs, impulsive acts seem unprovoked and inexplicable. Research has shown that alcohol consumption increases aggression, especially if the aggressor is egged on by a confederate (people consuming a placebo, thinking it is alcohol, do not aggress as much). Alcohol consumption is also one of the two best predictors of employees' aggression towards colleagues (the other is organisational injustice). Temperature also seems to affect aggression – one study in the city of Minneapolis found that assaults peaked at 25 degrees Celsius and declined thereafter.

We can become aggressive because of the substances we ingest, or because we become frustrated, or because we imitate aggression seen in others. Some famous experiments by Albert Bandura over thirty years ago found that children who had seen a person attack a doll were more likely to attack that doll than were children who hadn't observed this aggression. These studies, and those like them, seem to give credence to the hypothesis that exposure to film and TV violence can lead to increased violent/aggressive behaviour in the viewer. Evidence, however, is lacking and, in any event, reading the Bible and the Qur'an may be justifiably said to have provoked more acts of aggression than watching the entire *Starsky and Hutch* canon.

The opposite of aggression is helping, and humans, being generally co-operative in nature, are good at this although we are faced with dilemmas which can limit our prosocial behaviour. We might share the belief that drug users require rehabilitation or that more homes need to be built to meet demand, but we will object to a rehabilitation centre being built near where we live or if a piece of land in our town is ear-marked for new housing. Self-interest can usurp the general good but, often, give and take is necessary if long-term goals are to be achieved. For example, there is current controversy over depleting fish stocks – but these are replenishable if they are harvested properly. This, however, requires co-operation, and not competition.

Much was made, in the Summer of 2007, of people in the UK being afraid to intervene to stop people from committing anti-social behaviour such as vandalism, swearing, and assault. People fear retaliation and may not intervene to help another in trouble. But a variant of this phenomenon is not new. In 1964, in New York City, a young woman called Kitty Genovese was chased and repeatedly stabbed by an assailant who took thirty-five minutes to murder her. She screamed constantly. None of the thirty-eight people who heard her, and saw her from their apartment windows, helped. None made a call to the police. When later questioned, they could not explain their behaviour.

Parts of the media and the public were outraged: how could this be allowed to happen? Was society that cold and indifferent to the life of others? Actually, no. Psychologists who investigated the reasons why the bystanders did just that – stand by – suggested that it was precisely because so many people witnessed the assault that intervention did not occur.

Latane and Darley set up an experiment in which a person was asked to discuss personal problems about college life (this was a ruse) either alone or with a few others (sitting in different rooms; they did not exist but appeared as voices on tape). At one point, one of the discussants apparently had a seizure. Who do you think rushed out of the room to help? Yes, the person who was alone. Those who thought there were other witnesses did respond, but they were much slower to do so. These people were not indifferent – most were emotionally very concerned – but were in conflict over whether they should help. There seemed to be a perceived diffusion of responsibility which inhibited the individual acting spontaneously and immediately.

Other factors influence our ability to intervene – we are more likely to do this in a good, than bad, mood and if we are not in a hurry. One famous study of bystander intervention found that people in a hurry were less likely to help a person in distress. These people were theology students on their way to a lecture on the Good Samaritan.

If intelligence was problematic enough, psychologists have more or less given up trying to define love (although some have tried). Instead, they have focused on studying interpersonal attraction (from friendship to romantic and sexual relationships) and the factors which can facilitate, inhibit, or reduce this. Despite the hoary old adage, 'beauty is in the eye of the beholder', people do prefer physically attractive people – we believe they share our values, have a good personality, have more successful marriages (if married), and are more successful at work (and they may be all of these because of the reinforcement this blanket niceness covers them with).

One key predictor of attraction is proximity – we grow to like people to whom we are constantly exposed. Even in psychology experiments, brief interactions between participants led to these participants being rated as more attractive than those not encountered (although this is probably due to the fact that they did know a bit more about the participant – the way they looked, walked, talked, etc.). One researcher has even quantified interpersonal distance thus: up to half a metre is intimate; between 0.5 and 1.25m is personal; 1.25 and 4m is social; and 4 and 8m is public. People gaze longer at people they like (and high-status individuals are the recipients of longer gazes than they themselves give, unless they are trying to exert control over their underlings). The nature of proximity explains why long-distance relationships can be fractious and difficult to maintain: not only are you not physically close to each other any more but you become physically close to others.

We also tend to like people who like us. If we are told that another person likes us, we find that person more attractive (regardless of whether the statement is true). This seems to interact with self-esteem. Those with high self-esteem do not base attraction on reciprocal liking; those with low self-esteem do. We also dislike people who initially like us and then cool off and like more those people who grow to like us after perhaps initially disliking us, possibly because we derive pleasure from being liked or view people who are overly positive to start with as being undiscriminating.

The phrase 'opposites attract' is also another cliché that can be confined to the psychology dustbin. Most research indicates that we are attracted to people who are similar to us – in looks, interest, intelligence, and so on. People who are mismatched are more likely to break up. The more similar two people's attitudes are, the greater the attraction (this is actually called the 'law of attraction'). So, if your beau shares a similar love of obscure crooners such as Chikinki, you're off to a good start. If not, the omens are gloomy. The similarity effect extends to other relationships – such as friendships – as well as sexual ones, and similarity can extend to age, occupation, and ethnicity. Recent research, however, suggests that it is our ideal of a romantic partner and how well our partner matches it, rather than how similar we are, that leads to greater relationship satisfaction.

Predictors of relationship dissatisfaction are better documented. Few of us have not been in a relationship where we were unhappy with the other person – we grow bored, critical, dissatisfied, angry, frustrated at the lack of shared interests or goals. The more committed people are, the more likely the relationship is to last. Research published in the *Journal of*

Personality and Social Psychology has also shown that men's optimism is related to relationship success — the greater the optimism, the more secure the relationship. The guerrilla graffiti artist Banksy wrote that 'you know from the first moment you meet someone the reason why you will leave them'. That quirky, endearing foible in the first few weeks of the relationship becomes a persistent source of revulsion months or years later.

Factors promoting a successful relationship are personal dedication (mutual attraction), a sense of obligation to our partner, and external constraints that would make a break-up costly (financial and personal). Factors likely to subvert a relationship are the availability of alternative partners, an expectation that the relationship will fail, the need for a new life, constant arguments where a partner is continuously attacked, one partner having a narcissistic personality, and a lack of commitment. There are ways of dealing with all of these. If the relationship does fail, however, but it ends reasonably, one psychologist suggests a chronology of this breakdown: first, there is brooding, and the needling of a partner. This is followed by discussion of the relationship and its problems, acknowledgement that it is over and negotiation with friends that the right thing is being done, and, finally, 'grave dressing', where each partner puts a socially acceptable gloss on the termination.

In the next chapter, we'll consider the nature of emotion and emotional response a little further. What is an emotion? Can it be defined? How many are there? Are different systems in the brain responsible for different emotions? And what are emotions for?

9

Emotion, stress, and health

The word emotion comes from Latin meaning 'to stir up' or 'to agitate'. This definition is mercifully simple: reaching a scientific definition has been more difficult. One study found at least 556 words and phrases relating to emotion but, although there are disagreements, there is general consensus now that we exhibit at least six 'basic' emotions: sadness, disgust, happiness, surprise, anger, and fear; other emotions are combinations of these. In so far as they can be operationally defined, emotions are brief changes in feelings that occur in response to events or people (or recollections of both) which have motivational significance: they are responses to things that have motivated us. Their brevity distinguishes them from mood, which tends to be longer lasting. They may also be characterised by the activation of different neural and neurotransmitter pathways (we'll return to this later).

The proposition that there are six basic, universal emotions was based on cross-cultural research conducted by Ekman and Friesen in the 1960s and 1970s, although Charles Darwin had conducted a similar, if smaller scale, study of his own in the nineteenth century, concluding that universal expressions of emotions exist and that these were inherited. Ekman and Friesen argued that if remote tribes, which had not been exposed to Western culture, were able to identify emotional expressions in their own people and others then this would be evidence for the universality of emotion. This is what they found. The South Fore tribe of New Guinea was also able to select an appropriate emotion when asked to indicate what a person in a story was feeling. Research since has shown high degrees of accuracy in identifying the six basic emotions in a variety of cultures – the USA, Chile, Brazil, Argentina, Japan, and many others.

While some have regarded these findings as robust, others disagree. Some theorists argue that facial expressions are epiphenomena – fleeting and not remotely indicative of genuine emotion because facial expressions can be used to convey non-emotion information. We can also simulate emotion using facial expression. Smiling may be an indicator of joy, but could also be an indicator of sarcasm. Ekman would counter by saying that there are different muscles in the face involved in each type of smile. His Facial Action Coding System is a complex method of categorising facial expression based on a multitude of sometimes extremely subtle facial muscle changes that are not visible to the human eye but detectable by electrodes recording muscle contraction. In fact, there are two very different types of smile, one of which is genuine, the other false. The Duchenne smile, the genuine smile, involves activation of the orbicularis oculi muscles around the eye and the zygomatic muscles around the corners of the mouth; the false smile activates only the mouth muscles (a useful indicator of whether that joke has gone down well at a party).

Of course, we can express emotion in ways other than facial, through the body for example. 'One must sit with a sense of dignity and grandeur, like a mountain or a giant pine,' wrote Dogen, the Zen Buddhist Master in the thirteenth century, 'the innate dignity of man is physiologically manifested in his erect back, since he alone of all creatures has this capacity to hold his spinal column vertical.' Buddhist seating preferences aside, posture can affect behaviour and emotion (in terms of expression and experience). Darwin highlighted the evolutionary advantage of certain types of deportment – bodily movement and posture sent clear signals to members of the same and different species.

He also noted that pride was one of the more obviously signalled complex emotions – the upright posture indicated superiority over others. You can imagine the howls of despair echoing around Notre Dame. In a study published in *Cognition & Emotion* in 2007, men sitting upright were much more satisfied about their performance on a test than were women, a finding possibly explained by objectification theory – women are more self-conscious about their body image and any behaviour that emphasises a part of the body that creates such self-conscious-ness, therefore, will lead to their being more aware of this and judging it. Similar experiments have shown the same effect – women who perform cognitive tasks in a swimsuit perform less well than those wearing a jumper (or than men whose torso was naked).

Why do we emote?

Our response to negative and positive reinforcers and punish-ment is usually a transitory change in feeling, always accompa-nied by autonomic and central nervous system changes (more on these below). They are spontaneous or manufactured expres-sions of feeling or motivation. The manufacture of emotion is, as we all know, common: we know that our facial expressions may reveal what we feel and so we try and conceal our true feelings by being impassive or exaggerating our emotions (so, a poker player will be lapidary and someone who dislikes another's recent success but does not want to be seen as petty or jealous will offer exaggerated congratulations, gushing blandish-ments and fulsome facial expressions). The exaggeration or minimisation of an emotion is called modulation; when a person hides an emotion it is called masking. We tend to express more emotion in face-to-face encounters (and women generate more than men; there is not much of a difference between boys and girls), although this is culture dependent – the Japanese, for example, who have display rules which discourage public displays of emotion, tend to express fewer emotions in the company of others.

Another use for masking is deliberate deception. Which of the following do you think are the best indicators of a person not telling the truth? (You can select more than one.)

- Averting gaze
- Unnatural posture
- Scratching/touching parts of the body
- Playing with hair
- Placing hand on the mouth or eyes

If you chose one or more, you're in good company. A standard police manual of lie detection lists all of these as predictors. However, research shows that none of them are. People are very poor at detecting deception (unless it is really obvious), although specifically trained police officers and Secret Service agents (and, sometimes, criminals) tend to have the edge over untrained officers and members of the public. Participants who conclude that suspects are lying, when they aren't, usually cite the behaviours above. Some US companies, such as No Lie MRI Inc. and the Cephos Corporation, also claim that differences in brain activity can identify a liar although the evidence for this is poor.

Some police officers have criticised the methodology of behavioural studies – which usually involves participants watching videotapes of people and asking them whether the target is lying or telling the truth – arguing that interviewing a suspect is very different. In fact, research has shown that people who watch an interview are better able to tell the difference between liars and truth-tellers than are interviewers. Research suggests that the two most common predictors of deception in genuine liars are a high-pitched voice and a reduction in hand movement.

Although we can use our face to express genuine or false emotion in order to influence others, there is also evidence that the expression itself can lead to a change in our emotion (this is called the facial feedback hypothesis). Darwin had remarked that an augmentation of an emotional expression intensifies that emotion; a repression leads to its reduction. In one experimental demonstration, Strack and colleagues asked participants to watch cartoons as they held a pen either between their lips (as if sucking a straw) or between the teeth. Those whose expression had been inhibited (the teeth group) found the cartoons significantly less funny than did those in the uninhibited group (the lip group), suggesting that the failure to express emotion influenced the generation of emotion.

Mood and cognition

In an episode of *The Larry Sanders Show*, the head writer is castigated by the show's star and producer for enjoying himself too much with his new, energetic girlfriend because his jokes were becoming less and less funny (his energy seemed to have been channelled in a different direction). When she dumps him, his jokes get funnier. In art as in the lab, there is considerable evidence to suggest that extended emotion – mood – affects the way that we behave, and sometimes not in the way that seems obvious.

Very happy people tend to have stronger social and romantic relationships, spend less time alone, and are more agreeable and extraverted (although they do experience negative mood – it is not all untrammelled joy). The North American Nun study – a longitudinal study of ageing in American nuns – found that nuns with a more positive outlook lived longest. A study in which undergraduates' expressions of emotion were self-monitored three times a week for a month found that positive emotions dominated (thus suggesting that Freud's view that our normal mental state is unhappiness punctured by occasional jabs of happiness may be in need of revision). It is astonishing to think that even a photograph can reveal much about a person's emotional disposition. Harker and Keltner took photographs of women from their college year book and correlated the facial expressions with their personality – and others' assessment of their personality – later in life. Those who showed positive expressions in their photos expressed lower negative mood generally, had happy marriages and enhanced well-being.

Being in a positive mood, however, can have positive and negative cognitive effects. Research demonstrates that our mood often results in congruent behaviour – so exposure to an unpleasant odour, for example, leads people to recall more unhappy memories than happy ones whereas exposure to a pleasant odour has the opposite effect. A study in the journal *Physiology and Behavior* found that people in a happy mood rated foods as sweeter and more pleasant whereas those in an unhappy mood rated them as less pleasant and sweet. Experiments by Isen and her colleagues have found that people are willing to make large bets in a gambling task when they are in a positive mood but only when the chances of winning are high. People are also more likely to make riskier (real-life) decisions while in a good mood. Isen found that a positive mood was associated with a beneficial effect on creative problem-solving (the task was to support a lighted candle on a door using some drawing pins, some matches in a matchbox, and a candle).

Others have found that a negative mood interferes with a task in which people were asked to look for contradictions in a passage of prose, presumably because intrusive and irrelevant thoughts interfered with the task. If this is so, some tasks will be impaired by a positive mood because the thoughts – although positive – may compete with resources needed to complete the task. This is what a study by Mike Oaksford and colleagues found when they measured people's performance on a forward planning task. Other tasks, which presumably did not require resources that would be competed for, showed no impairment in performance. A negative (unhappy) mood can also be beneficial to some types of cognition. A recent study from the University of New South Wales found that people who were in a negative mood were more likely to produce persuasive interpersonal messages in support of, or against, a particular position than were those in a good mood: the negative mood seemed to result in greater focus and more concrete information processing.

The biology of emotion: expression vs. recognition

Some neuroscientists have suggested that if there are discrete, 'basic' emotions then it follows that there are different systems and structures in the brain that subserve these different emotions (sadness is the opposite of happiness, for example, and so would be unlikely to be characterised by the same neural 'signature'). There is some evidence for this and the regions of the brain that are thought to be involved in the expression of emotion are the orbitofrontal cortex, the insula, and the amygdala.

It is important to distinguish between the two processes of expression and recognition. Recognising an emotion recruits different brain regions and processes to those involved in experiencing an emotion: you can identify a happy face without necessarily feeling happy. Evidence suggests that the right hemisphere is better than the left at identifying emotions in sights (words, photographs) and sounds (voices). This superiority gave rise to the right-for-emotion hypothesis of emotion which stated that the right hemisphere was responsible for emotional processing. It isn't – it is better at recognition but it contributes with the left hemisphere (and specific parts of the left hemisphere) to emotional expression.

Fear

The most widely studied emotion in the laboratory is fear. This is because it can be easily conditioned and the behaviours associated with it are stereotypical and predictable. Work with rodents, for example, has found two routes in the brain that lead to the learning and expression of fear. In a typical classical conditioning experiment, Joseph LeDoux and colleagues in the USA paired a conditioned stimulus – a flash of light/a sound – with an unconditioned stimulus – an electric shock – so that the organism learned to fear a previously unfeared stimulus (light/sound). Le Doux found that if you severed a pathway from the relevant sensory cortex to the amygdala, this interfered with learning, and fear conditioning did not take place. The study confirms the importance of the amygdala to our appreciation of socially or physically dangerous stimuli which present a threat. Animals with lesioned amygdalae become tame; when injected with an excitatory drug, they become fearful and agitated. Studies of humans with amygdala damage show that they are unable to recognise or sometimes express the emotion of fear, or identify social or cognitive expressions in faces (the positive emotions are unaffected) such as hostility, friendliness, and pensiveness: fear in voices and faces goes unidentified, as does the identification of negative emotions in people. Some neuroimaging studies have shown that the more intense the facial expression of fear, the greater the activation in the amygdala (especially in the left). However, the amygdala is involved in many behaviours (and it has many parts) and scanning studies also show that it becomes active when viewing positive visual stimuli.

Happiness and sadness

One of the most important regions for expressing positive and negative emotion is the orbitofrontal cortex (OFC), the part of the brain located just above the eye sockets. People receiving pleasant stimulation – such as smelling pleasant vanilla or being stroked by a velvet glove – show activation in the OFC. But perhaps the most famous illustration of its role in emotion was seen in an American railroad worker from the nineteenth century. Phineas Gage's job was to ensure that terrain for railway tracks was flat. To do this, large boulders needed to be removed by inserting gun powder into a hole in the rock, pushing the powder in with a tamping iron (a long rod) covered with cloth, and detonating a charge. On 13 September 1848, Gage forgot to cover the end of the iron with cloth and the iron made contact with the powder which caused an explosion. The explosion sent the iron hurtling through his left cheek and through the top of his head, destroying much of his left OFC. When Gage's physician attended the scene, he reported that Gage's eyeball was dangling by a nerve but that Gage himself was conscious and surprisingly sentient and aware. It was only afterwards that his behaviour seemed to change. Before the injury, he was regarded as conscientious, hard-working, dutiful, and well-behaved. After the injury, he became slovenly, slothful, boorish, and started drinking and swearing. According to colleagues, 'he was no longer Gage'.

This disinhibition following injury to the OFC is now well documented. Another patient, EVR, first described by Antonio Damasio and Daniel Tranel in the mid-1980s, showed similar changes to Phineas Gage after removal of part of the left OFC due to tumour growth. EVR was a hard-working accountant, happily married, church-going, an apparent model of American citizenship. After surgery, his behaviour approximated that of Gage. The remarks of patients who have undergone OFC surgery highlight similar changes: they feel less inhibited, more impulsive, regard others' feelings indifferently. Given that the OFC and the frontal cortex allow us to monitor our ongoing behaviour and prevent us from behaving impulsively, these consequences following injury are perhaps predictable. The social problems seen in frontal lobe patients tend to be more common when damage is to the right lobe.

In healthy individuals, the left and right frontal lobes may be differentially involved in the expression of different types of emotion. A series of EEG experiments by Richard Davidson and his colleagues at the University of Wisconsin have shown greater activation in the left side of the brain when people view positive film clips but more on the right side when they watch negative film clips. Even baseline EEG activation predicted emotional response to these films. In one experiment, those individuals with higher left than right EEG activation at baseline responded more positively to positive films. Individuals with higher left than right frontal EEG at rest also feel more positively after a thirty-minute session on a treadmill. The left-right frontal difference has been extended to many stimuli. People listening to pleasant music show more left and less right frontal EEG whereas people listening to unpleasant music show the opposite pattern; people who report generally better well-being show greater left frontal EEG activation.

The reason for this may be that the frontal lobe regulates motivational tendencies, specifically the motivation to approach or withdraw: we approach things we like (and this is reflected in more left, less right frontal activation) but withdraw from those we dislike (reflected in more right, less left frontal activation).

Anger and disgust

The OFC is also implicated in anger. One part of it, the anterior cingulate cortex, and the right OFC became more active when watching faces of increasingly intense anger. Its role in express-ing anger is also shown in EEG experiments. In terms of approach and withdrawal, anger seems like a negative emotion but it makes us want to approach (to aggress against the source of anger). Some psychologists have suggested that anger, in this sense, is a positive emotion, because people who get angry like being angry. One study found that those who described themselves as angry showed more left-sided activation, thus supporting this view of anger and perhaps suggesting that the left-right difference reflects motivation tendencies rather than emotional responses specifically.

Disgust has also been found to recruit the OFC. People who watch and rate disgusting images show activation in the left OFC and the amygdala, amongst other regions. There is also some evidence that patients with the motor disorder, Huntington's Disease, are specifically unable to identify disgust in facial expressions but recent research suggests that this impair-ment extends to other negative stimuli too.

Theories of emotion

One of the earliest scientific explanations of emotion was independently suggested by an American psychologist and a Danish physiologist. The James–Lange theory, as it is known, suggested that emotion-provoking situations produced physio-logical responses (such as increased heart rate, sweating) and behavioural ones (e.g. clenched fists) which are fed back to the brain. This sensory feedback is what constitutes a feeling of emotion. The theory fails, however, because the mechanism it suggests is too slow: visceral changes are too sluggish to be able to reflect swift emotional changes. A different model, proposed by Schacter and Singer, suggested that emotion arose from our perception of physiological changes and the assessment of the situation we are in. For example, if we are given a shot of adrenalin and either told that we might experience bodily changes or not and then put in situations where we are made angry or where we observe somebody behaving stupidly, we experience less of an emotional change if we have been told about the effect of the adrenalin. When people were given a sham pill they were told would make their heart pound and were then given electric shocks, those given the pill tolerated stronger shocks than did a control group. Curiously, when asked what they thought about during the experiment, those given the pill did not think about it or its effects.

Other models stress the importance of cognition to emotion. For example, Lazarus's model emphasises the importance of primary appraisal – where we initially evaluate the environment for positive or negative stimuli; and secondary appraisal – where we evaluate how best to cope with this environment. A later version of the model refined these processes – does the environment help us to meet/hinder our goal? Does the environment have any consequences for our self-esteem? How might we cope with the environment and the consequences of acting on our assessment of the environment? A similar model argues that emotions are generated by the positive and negative attributions we make to the environment and others' behaviour. Some emotional responses are primitive and automatic; others are attribution-dependent. So, for example, if you had been assaulted by a certain type of person and you were approached one night by a very similar type of person, you would make a negative attribution to that person and experience fear and/or anger.

Another model assumes that the environment we encounter presents us with multiple goals and the importance of emotion is in prioritising these goals. Other models see emotions as means of helping us to adapt or survive, allowing us to react to the environment using a limited behavioural repertoire. They are 'action tendencies' because they arise from our appraisal of the environment and prepare us for acting on it.

Stress

Lazarus's model, above, was originally devised to explain our response to stressors – aversive stimuli that are perceived as threatening or endangering our well-being or ability to achieve a goal. They can come in many forms – from a job interview and sitting an examination to serious stressors like illness or physical trauma such as being held at gunpoint or raped. Stressors cause stress – a physiological, behavioural, emotional, and cognitive response which allows us to adapt to the environment, either by fleeing or staying put and fighting. The term was popularised by the Austrian-born Canadian endocrinologist Hans Selye in the 1950s. People were used to talking about 'strain' rather than stress but Selye actually used the correct term, borrowed from engineering, because it refers to the pressure placed on an object causing it to change shape (strain is a measure of the degree of change produced by stress).

Physiologically, our response to stressors is predictable: heart rate, blood pressure, adrenalin, and blood sugar levels rise, blood vessels constrict, blood flow is directed to major organs, breathing becomes deeper, digestion stops, and perspiration increases. All of these cause alertness and ready the body for action: either fleeing or fighting. Selye's research, using animals, suggested that chronic stressors produce three stress reactions (the process was summed by the term, 'general adaptation syndrome'). The first stage is alarm, where our resistance to the stressor drops and we experience 'shock'. The second stage is resistance, where continued exposure leads to normal functioning being resumed. Finally, if the stressor continues to be present after this, the organism enters the exhaustion stage. The ability to adapt and to resist plummets. This is the stage that is dangerous to health.

While evidence to support the stage-process nature of the model is not conclusive – there are, for example, individual differences which influence our response to stressors, and some people are characteristically more resilient or hardy than others – there is considerable research indicating that continued exposure to chronic stressors affects health, especially the normal functioning of our immune system and the cardiovascular system. During stress, various chemicals are produced from the adrenal glands that ready the body for action – adrenalin, for example. It also produces a steroid called cortisol which helps break down protein for conversion to glucose, which the body needs as an energy source, and makes fats available as energy. Prolonged secretion, however, can be harmful – it affects memory and thinking, and produces changes in physiology.

Stressors affect the immune system by reducing the levels of antibodies available to fight infection. The job of the immune system is to protect the body from infection: invading bacteria, fungus, viruses, and so on. Antibodies are proteins that recognise antigens – other proteins which appear on the surface of invading bacteria and eliminate bacteria, either by recruiting other cells to kill off invading organisms or by secreting chemicals that will do the same (allergies arise when an antigen produces an over-reaction in the immune system). One type of antibody is called secretory immunoglobulin A or sIgA and has been widely studied by psychologists in the lab because it can be extracted fairly easily from saliva. Feeling that you have a lower quality of life than others is associated with low sIgA, as is experiencing examination stress and caring for medically demanding relatives. For example, Kielcolt-Glaser and her colleagues found that the degree of wound healing was slower in relatives who cared for people with Alzheimer's Disease than in matched controls. One recent review found that caregivers' levels of stress hormones were, on average, twenty-three per cent higher than those of non-caregivers and their antibody level fifteen per cent lower. However, less chronic stress (acute stress) can lead to an increase in antibodies which suggests that some stress can be beneficial. Also, in situations where the support is not constant, such as the support married people give each other, people show reduced risk of mortality.

The compromise to the immune system during feelings of extreme stress might suggest that we contract more infections in this state. Research supports this: upper respiratory infection has been shown to follow undesirable events or a decline in desirable ones. In one extraordinary but elegantly executed study, researchers exposed individuals to two common cold viruses and correlated infection and the development of a cold with personality and life events. Forty per cent developed a cold and these were most likely to have endured chronic life stressors for at least a month. A separate study found that the more sociable a person is, the less likely he or she is to develop a cold.

Various factors can accelerate or protect against these effects: optimism, for example, a disposition to believe in positive outcomes, is consistently associated with good coping and with prevention of ill-health, as is conscientiousness and having a positive emotional disposition (being optimistic, generous, curious). Procrastination, however, is not. Some have suggested that people with Type A personality – characterised by excessive competitiveness, impatience, and hostility – are more stress-prone than Type B personalities (who are less competitive and hostile, and are more patient). A few studies, for example, have associated Type A behaviour with increased risk for cardiovascular heart disease. When Type A personalities are competing against others, their heart rate rises significantly, which may present a risk factor.

Work stress can lead to ill-health – the Whitehall study of civil servants and coronary heart disease (CHD), for example, has found that the lower the grade in the service, the more likely the death from CHD. A study of absenteeism in Swedish employees found that male professions with the highest levels were shop assisting, repair work, and welding (logging and mechanics were the lowest); female professions at the top of the list were shop work, nursing, and secretarial work. In Japan it is thought that working in excess of 11 hours a day can lead to 'karoshi' (fatal heart attacks). Unemployment is also an important predictor of stress (although some recent research suggests that being in a job you hate is just as stressful as losing a job you like). Self-esteem decreases and depression increases due to the new levels of isolation and lack of structure and social interaction. Loneliness has also been associated with reduced antibody levels – first-year students who reported being most lonely and had the smallest social networks showed the lowest antibody response. They also had more circulating cortisol, slept less well, and experienced more negative emotions.

Finally, harbouring grievances seems not at all conducive to good health. A study published in *Psychological Science* in 2001 found that people who expressed unforgiving thoughts about others had higher blood pressure, felt greater negative emotion, and had accelerated heart rate. It really does seem better to forgive and forget (and probably easier said than done).

Psychological interventions to deal with the effects of stress have met with modest success when the stress has not been caused by illness (they seem ineffective for this type of stress). Disclosure interventions – where people write about their stressful experiences – have been quite successful in enhancing immune system response. Problem-focused coping relies on a person fixing a stressful problem by altering the nature of the problem directly; emotion-focused coping is directed towards the emotional response to the stressor, so the person might be told to engage in relaxation techniques or to seek social interaction (social support is one of the best predictors of successful coping). A person might also engage in a re-appraisal of a threat so that it becomes less stressful – an advancing lion is obviously something that should be stressful, but speaking in front of people should not be. Another technique, called stress inoculation training, aims to head off the effects of stress before stressors are encountered. By equipping people with the coping skills necessary to deal with negative life events, this should reduce levels of stress.

The psychology of healthy – and unhealthy – living

Barely a year goes by without a news report suggesting that some local health authority or primary care trust is refusing treatment to a patient because he or she is either morbidly obese or a chain-smoker. Jamie Oliver highlighted the scandal of the kind of reconstituted detritus British school children eat for lunch. We are, it appears, getting fatter, living on a diet of lard, and sitting all day in front of re-runs of Jerry Springer, slowly mentally and physically decomposing. PlayStations are preferred over play areas, assuming there are any of those left after local authorities have sold them off to property developers.

Health psychology is one of the newer branches of psychology and aims to promote and maintain health, identify and help prevent risk factors for illness, and to advise on health care/government policy. Unlike clinical psychology, its focus is on bodily illness rather than mental illness. Recently, health psychologists have helped us to understand better the motivating factors behind cigarette smoking and stopping, for example, and the predictors of weight gain and motivated weight loss, amongst other behaviours.

Cigarette smoking

Unlike food (and its excessive consumption), we don't need cigarettes to survive. Yet, some people enjoy smoking, despite the physical dangers of some of the chemicals in tobacco, and the generally disgusting and intrusive nature of the habit. An estimated twenty-five million deaths in the European Union (EU) were attributable to smoking between 1950 and 2000. That is a lot of coffins. Latest statistics suggest that around thirty-five per cent of men and twenty-five per cent of women in the EU smoke – the number of women smokers has decreased in Denmark, the Netherlands, Sweden, and the UK but increased in Greece, Portugal, and Spain.

Data reported in 1998 found that China consumed 1643 billion cigarettes that year; the next most voracious consumers were the USA, Japan, Russia, and Indonesia. Smoking is thought to cause a third of all cancers. Concerned by this, governments have taken the fairly draconian step of banning smoking (but usually only in public places such as offices, restaurants, clubs, etc.), as well as banning advertising – California in 1998, Ireland in 2004, Scotland in 2006, and the rest of the UK in 2007. Despite initial protestations, the ban in California did not dent restaurant and bar sales – in fact, they increased from $2.1 billion to $2.7 billion. The most well-off are those most likely to quit smoking; the less well-educated are those most likely to continue smoking. Smoking also seems to have undesirable associated side effects – smokers tend to eat more fatty food, have lower fruit and veg intake, engage in less physical activity, and drink more alcohol.

What prompts people to smoke in the first place? Imitation and peer pressure during adolescence are strong influences, especially the latter, as is alcohol consumption with one or more friends. A study of 4035 participants found that smoking increased from adolescence to adulthood with a slight decrease in smoking initiation in the mid-twenties and none in later adulthood. Non-quitters were likely to have parents who were smokers and were less well-educated. Boys tend to take up smoking sooner and girls' smoking has been associated with a belief that it will ward off eating disorders. One study found that girl smokers were likely to be overweight in adolescence but underweight in middle age.

Much has been said about the addictive nature of smoking and it is: smokers develop a tolerance to it and become physically dependent on it. Tolerance means that the CNS needs larger doses to satisfy itself (or to create the initial, pleasurable effects). Without the drug, people will feel anxious, experience discomfort, withdrawal symptoms, sweating, and so on. There is also 'psychological' tolerance for the active drug in tobacco – nicotine. That is, tobacco use continues because of the pleasurable effects it produces. Changes in the CNS produced by nicotine include stimulation of certain neurotransmitter receptor types. The effect of this is to increase heart rate, decrease body temperature, change hormone release, and release adrenalin. It also causes the release of the neurotransmitter dopamine – a drug that is tremendously reinforcing. Smoking can continue because these effects and the withdrawal effects are strong – around sixty per cent of quitters re-start, to escape unpleasant withdrawal symptoms. Nicotine is not the chemical that causes most of the physical problems – the combination of nicotine and the carbon monoxide and tars in tobacco is what causes deprivation of oxygen to the heart, for example.

How can smokers quit? In 1996, a survey of eighty Australian 'smoking experts' recommended that the most successful smoking reduction strategies would be increased taxes, TV campaigning, smoke-free areas, and an advertising ban, in that order. In isolation, however, these strategies have been found to be relatively ineffective. It is the combination of strategies that appears to reduce smoking. In terms of physical intervention, nicotine patches (invented by a psychologist, Frank Etscorn), and gum, where the nicotine release is gradually reduced, meet with equivocal success – thirteen per cent and eleven per cent, respectively. Lapsing can arise when smokers drink alcohol and when they are in situations where others smoke. Intensive counselling for smoking cessation in seriously ill people (those with CHD) can be effective. One study of 160 patients randomly assigned participants to two groups: one received general advice and the other received more intensive intervention including thirty-minute inpatient counselling sessions, an outpatient visit, and telephone counselling. The latter group were more likely to quit. Telephone counselling can also be successful in helping 'healthy' smokers to quit.

Obesity

Like smoking, obesity is difficult to overcome. Obesity, in Western countries, is defined as having body fat that exceeds twenty-five per cent of bodyweight in women and eighteen per cent in men. This is measured using the Body Mass Index (BMI) which takes weight in kilograms and divides it by height in metres squared. To be clinically obese, a person must have a BMI of $30kg/m^2$. Around sixty per cent of American adults are estimated to be either overweight or obese and only a minority of adults are thought to have the desired BMI of between 18.5 to 24.9. You can measure your own BMI by going to www.shapeup.org. According to the US Centre for Disease Control and the National Cancer Institute, around 112,000 deaths in 2000 were attributable to obesity, and the US spends around $92 billion a year treating obese or overweight patients.

Obesity can be caused by habit such as how much food we think is right to eat – when we are young and active we can eat this amount but, as we age and become less active, the same amount makes us put on weight; or by metabolism – the process whereby energy is produced from nutrients. Some people are more fuel-efficient than others and this seems to have a hereditary basis (as one researcher has said, 'genes load the gun, the environment pulls the trigger'). In more active times, an efficient metabolism was an advantage; in less active times, readily available food can promote obesity. When people go on crash diets and starve themselves, this affects their metabolism: it becomes more efficient. This means that during the starvation, weight loss occurs, but when the dieting stops, the weight is regained. In fact, the more often this happens, the faster the weight gain and the slower the weight loss (the so-called yo-yo effect).

The most commonly prescribed interventions for obesity are: increased physical exercise, reduced fat and sugar intake, and a will to maintain both. The most drastic intervention is bariatric surgery where layers of fat are removed – this has side-effects but is effective; patients can also undergo a gastric bypass where a pouch is connected to a part of the intestine (the jejunum) bypassing the stomach. This does lead to sustained weight loss a decade after surgery. Weight loss is only successful if people are motivated to lose weight and they set realistic goals. Until recently, programmes were designed to make participants reach their ideal weight, rather than reach a weight that would reduce the risk of illness. So, a loss of fifteen per cent – which is effective – was seen as unacceptable because participants wanted to lose more (twenty to thirty-five per cent).

People find giving up food difficult, especially during holidays such as Christmas and New Year. If people actively self-monitor what they eat, they can restrict their intake. This is even more successful if they are helped by receiving literature and phone calls from researchers. Weight loss maintenance is initially successful – people will lose about nine per cent – but once the structured nature of an intervention programme stops, people can put on as much as third of their weight. Portion control can help prevent this, as can adhering to a physical exercise regime. Studies have shown that people who exercise at home maintain their weight loss better than those who go to gyms.

Of course, obesity is not the only diet-related condition that can impair physical and psychological health. Other eating disorders, such as anorexia nervosa and bulimia nervosa, also have serious consequences for long-term health. Although anorexia literally means loss of appetite, the disorder is characterised by a reduction in eating rather than appetite (which is intact). It affects between 0.5 to 1% of the population, mainly young women but, increasingly, young men. Individuals become preoccupied with food and its preparation and have an extreme fear of becoming obese. Anorexic people consistently underestimate their body shape and weight and have extreme body image distortion. People with bulimia nervosa gorge themselves periodically with highly calorific food (binging) and some follow this up by vomiting (purging). They are less concerned than anorexic people with food but are obsessed by body image. It occurs in between one and three per cent of the population but recent data from the UK, USA, and the Netherlands suggest that the incidence is declining.

Body dissatisfaction is a key risk factor in the development of eating disorders and this is significantly higher in young women than it is in middle-aged women. One theory – self-objectification theory, described in the emotion section earlier – argues that most Western cultures regard the female body as being one that is viewed and evaluated. There is a tendency in women to monitor their appearance, judging it as others (mostly men) would view it. Noting that the body does not meet the ideal – or the perceived notion of an ideal – the woman becomes dissatisfied about her appearance. One consequence of such monitoring is increased anxiety and shame about the body. Ultimately, it could be argued, such monitoring leads to eating disorder, anxiety, and sexual dysfunction. There is some evidence to support the theory: young women are overly concerned with their appearance and with how others view them. An Australian study of 322 women aged between twenty and eighty-four found that although body dissatisfaction was consistent across all ages, self-objectification, habitual body monitoring, appearance anxiety, and symptoms of eating disorders were greatest in the younger sample and decreased with age. One source of women's body dissatisfaction is the media. Thin women are portrayed as paragons of their kind: they are healthy, better-looking, attract the most desirable men, and so on. Women who watch thin media images of other women express a significantly greater negative body image than when watching average-sized women, especially if the viewing women are under nineteen years old and are concerned with their body weight (women with eating disorders report less anxiety about their body when watching magazine advertisements featuring average-sized models).

Exercise

That obesity has become so prevalent in developed countries is probably attributable to our increasingly sedentary lifestyles and lack of exercise. Exercisers seem to live longer, are at less risk of cardiovascular disease, have less body fat, and are less susceptible to stressors. Even walking seems to prevent us from falling into an early grave (as it were). A study of sixty-one- to eighty-year non-smokers found that 21.5% of those who walked two miles a week died within twelve years, but 43% of non-walkers did. Walking was also associated with reduced CHD.

The type of exercise that benefits the heart is aerobic – running, walking, cycling, swimming. It increases blood flow and respiration, thus strengthening the lungs and heart. There is evidence that it can also help people cope better with stress, alleviate negative mood, and reduce anxiety, but the psychological effects may depend on the intensity of the exercise (mood can improve after aerobic dance and football, but not tennis or bowling for this reason). One study of twenty- to twenty-five-year-olds found that ten minutes of energetic cycling was sufficient to improve mood (no further improvement occurred after twenty minutes) whereas another, in which twenty-four-year-old students ran on a treadmill where the speed and workload was gradually increased, found an initial increase in arousal, then a further increase coupled with negative mood as the task became more difficult, but an elevation in positive mood one minute after stopping.

Alcohol

Of all the drugs described in this book, the most widely used and abused is alcohol. Abuse means that consumption can threaten the consumer's safety and well-being or that of others. Alcoholism describes an addiction to ethanol, the chemical in drinks which affects the CNS, and can lead to cirrhosis of the liver, poor nutrition, sexual dysfunction, cognitive impairment, increased anxiety, irritability, and aggression and, more generally, relationship fracture, decreased productivity, and absenteeism from work. Men alcoholics outnumber women. Alcohol suppresses neural activity which allows the inhibitory control we normally have on behaviour; we become more relaxed – socially, cognitively, and motorically (our speech becomes slurred and we lose co-ordination). Alcohol is quickly absorbed into the blood stream and is affected by body weight and muscle mass (as well as whether we have a full stomach). The liver metabolises alcohol at a constant rate but when blood alcohol level reaches 0.3–0.4%, we lose consciousness. Moderate amounts of alcohol, however, may be protective (against CHD, for example), although such studies are correlational.

We learn to drink in the same way that some people smoke – through imitation and peer pressure. Drinking in youth represents maturity, independence (or rebelliousness), and pleasure. In adults, our daily experiences and mood influence intake – the greater the negative experiences we experience in a day, the more likely we are to drink, and drink alone.

In this chapter, you've read about some of the physical and psychological factors that can affect physical and, indirectly, psychological health. In the next chapter, we'll consider what happens when psychological health is completely impaired.

10
Mental illness

What is 'abnormal' about 'abnormal psychology'?

In 1998, a poll published for European Brain Day found that sixty-one per cent of respondents thought that anorexia nervosa and bulimia nervosa were all in the mind and ninety-two per cent thought that these disorders were curable and that sufferers brought these on themselves. Almost half thought depression was avoidable and also 'all in the mind'.

The psychology of mental health is woefully misunderstood by those not directly affected by it and by those who do not study or research it. It is an uncomfortable topic. Despite the brilliantly laudable attempts at undermining the stigma attached to mental illness, exemplified by Stephen Fry's BBC documentary on bipolar disorder and Lewis Wolpert and Kay Jamison's autobiographical books on depression and manic-depression, the stigma remains. The embarrassment is compounded by the ignorance of the nature of mental illness, often not helped by the confusing proclamations of diagnosticians, psychiatrists, and psychologists themselves who have fetishistically classified odd behaviour as illness, and because no one type of mental illness ever presents itself in a 'clear-cut' form (and many co-exist). Several studies have demonstrated that being labelled as mentally ill – even when people aren't – can lead to stigmatisation. One study from the 1970s played a videotape of a man to a group of psychoanalysts, half of whom were told the man was a job applicant and half that he was a patient. Those told he was a patient rated him as more disturbed and less well-adjusted. Labelling also has another problem – the label cannot explain a disorder, it can only describe it.

Misunderstandings also surround specific disorders. Depression is not simply feeling low or being in a sad mood, for example. It is a relentless, debilitating illness that stops you from living. There is no point telling a depressed person to pull their socks up – he or she is not stupid or incapable, but trapped in a grey straitjacket of hopelessness, restlessness, and helplessness, often caused by a traumatic event (or series of traumatic events) but, sometimes, by no identifiable external cause at all. As Clive James put it:

> The capacity for happiness works the same way as the capacity for misery, in that it refuses to be relative. If you have made a loved one miserable, it's useless to tell them that many thousands of people are currently dying by violence. In fact, it's another form of violence to say so. Misery can seldom be reasoned away.

Abnormal psychology is the branch of psychology concerned with the diagnosis, understanding, and treatment of mental illness. The term abnormal has made some commentators uncomfortable but it simply refers to an extreme departure from the norm (in this sense Stephen Hawking, J.K. Rowling, Paul McCartney, and Richard Feynman are also abnormal). The current thinking, however, is that it is not the departure from the norm that is important but whether the behaviour is maladaptive and prevents the person from functioning adequately. Mental illness can be a disorder of thought, feeling, or behaviour that is deviant and which has cognitive, environ-mental, genetic, or biological causes. Some are reactions to events; others have a more complex causation (or 'aetiology') involving hereditary factors or neurotransmitter dysfunction. Mental illness is common and widespread. According to the US National Institute of Mental Health, an estimated 26.2 million

Americans (a quarter of the population) suffer from a diagnosable mental illness. Depression is the most commonly diagnosed illness of any kind in the world.

Although not the only one, the dominant model of mental illness is the medical model – this views mental illness as a disorder of the brain and nervous system which can be treated like physical illnesses. Many disorders can be so treated – schizophrenia and depression, for example, provided that some psychological therapy is provided alongside the pharmacological therapy. Others, however, appear to have no physical cause – for these, there are different interpretations involving family relations, or maladaptive thinking based on inaccurate perception of environmental events. One modification to the medical model also suggests that some people have a predisposition – through genetics and early experiences – to develop a mental illness but a later, environmental trigger is required before it manifests itself (the diasthesis-stress model).

Classification of mental illness

The two systems used to classify mental illness are the *Diagnostic and Statistical Manual of the American Psychiatric Association-IV (DSM-IV)* and the World Health Organisation's *International Classification of Diseases – 10*, with the former being more widely used because it specifically focuses on mental disorder. These are essentially detailed manuals for the diagnosis of mental disorder. DSM-IV includes 350 disorders that appear across cultures (it also lists twenty-five disorders that are culture-specific) and describes psychological conditions using five criteria, or axes. Axis 1 describes the major clinical syndromes such as substance abuse, schizophrenia, anxiety, mood, sleep, sexual and eating disorders, and others. Axis 2 describes personality disorders such as anti-social behaviour or narcissism. Axes 3 to 5 describe aspects of the person's life and development (such as the degree of stress experienced in the last year; social and occupational functioning; and physical health). Axis 5 measures whether a person's quality of life has been impaired by the disorder (measured on a 100-point global assessment of functioning scale – 100 represents no impairment; 10 represents a disorder that could cause the individual harm).

Critics, such as Thomas Szasz, claim that such classification has done individuals more harm than good. Labelling relieves the person of responsibility, discharging it to medical practitioners. (Szasz wrote a very famous polemic, *The Myth of Mental Illness*, on the topic.) Even DSM's defenders acknowledge that it has become bloated in recent revisions, labelling odd or eccentric behaviour as deviant or abnormal – sleep disorders were not considered mental disorders in DSM-III, for example, but are in DSM-IV. It is as if, in one critic's words, they became disorders over night. There is another 'basket' category in DSM called 'sexual disorder not otherwise specified', which is a catch-all category for any disorder not described in the manual. DSM-V is currently being planned and the emphasis in the future may be on viewing mental disorders as continua or dimensions, rather than as discrete categories of abnormal behaviour.

Treating mental illness

The history of treatments in psychiatry is not glorious. Many were painful – trepanning, for example, which entailed drilling a hole in the skull to allow evil spirits to escape. In the eighteenth century, many people believed that peculiar behaviour was attributable to witchcraft. A sixteenth-century physician, Johann Wier, was one of the first to challenge this belief, suggesting that individuals who were being tortured or burned for their behaviour were suffering from mental illness. In the

1930s, Edgar Moniz famously destroyed parts of the frontal lobe to reduce aggression and anti-social behaviour (this involved inserting an ice-pick-like device called a leucotome into a nostril, pushing it right into the frontal lobe and moving it back and forth until the tissue was destroyed).

Modern treatment began in earnest in the late eighteenth/early nineteenth century and the first textbook on mental illness, which categorised disorders and described their symptoms, was published in 1883 by Emil Kraeplin (this was the forerunner to DSM – some of Kraeplin's original categories can still be found in it). Current treatment approaches can be divided into four main types: psychodynamic, humanistic/psychotherapy, cognitive-behavioural, and biological.

Psychodynamic approaches

Based on Freud's psychoanalysis, early psychodynamic approaches involved providing the client with insight into their unconscious thoughts and desires. In Freud's words, 'to lift the veil of amnesia which hides the earliest years of childhood and to bring to conscious memory the manifestations of early infantile sexual life which are contained in them'. Insights are provided by the client's thoughts, the interpretation of dreams, memories (or what can't be remembered), emotion, and manner of speech, usually by engaging in free association (speaking freely and without embarrassment). Over a period of years, a patient would become less inhibited in what they spoke about.

Psychoanalysis is now referred to as 'psychodynamic therapy' to separate the historical version from its current incarnation, which places less importance on sexual behaviour and more on interpersonal experiences. People who undergo psychodynamic therapy are usually self-selecting – they are intelligent, articulate, and motivated (and also quite well off, given the length of time the therapy takes). It is rarely the first or second choice of treatment for serious mental illness.

Humanistic/psycho- therapies

Humanistic therapies believe in helping people achieve their maximum potential – clients have self-worth and are inherently good. Carl Rogers developed one of the first therapies in the 1940s, calling it client-centred therapy because the client was in charge and decided what to talk about and what could be done. Rogers believed that most people's problems stemmed from incongruence – their perception of what they are compared with what they would like to be did not match. Therapy was a means of getting closer to the ideal self. The therapist does not judge the client in any way (a process called unconditional positive regard) and does not direct the client. However, when Rogers's sessions were taped, Rogers was found to reinforce positively much of what the patient said (thus directing the client), a finding he acknowledged.

Other forms of psychotherapy include group therapy and family/couples therapy. In group therapy, two or more people meet with the therapist to discuss problems (it originated after the Second World War when members of the armed forces returned with psychological problems but there were not enough psychotherapists to meet the demand). An advantage is that if several members of the group comment in a similar way on a person's behaviour, the person is more likely to accept this comment. Knowing that others share the same problem can also be comforting. The format of these sessions varies: sometimes they are just lectures, and the group asks questions; other times, there is significant interaction between members.

Sometimes, a client's family is part of the environment that has caused his or her difficulties and so family therapy brings together members and observes how they interact. The therapist collects data about these interactions – where people sit, who interrupts who, who looks at who, etc. Members may be asked to act out behaviours so they can see how their maladaptiveness has caused the client's disorder. Therapy can also occur in relationships. Couples therapy normally involves resolving some conflict – arguments about money, jobs, housework, sexual impotence, or infidelity.

Does psychotherapy work? It is certainly one of the most popular treatments for the less serious mental illnesses. An analysis of studies published between 1990 and 1999 found that half of clients showed improvement in mental health but this was not sustained two years later (especially if the person was depressed or anxious). Psychotherapy was most effective for panic disorder (see below); forty-six per cent of patients improved.

Cognitive behavioural therapies

Behavioural therapies assume that people learn to behave maladaptively just as they learn to behave adaptively. One of the therapy's pioneers, Joseph Wolpe, suggested that we learn to fear some stimuli that are not themselves painful because we have learned to associate the stimuli with pain via classical or operant conditioning. To combat phobia, for example, one of his techniques involved gradually introducing the feared object to the client. First, relaxation training would be administered; then a hierarchy of anxiety-related stimuli would be introduced. So, if a person feared spiders, the clinician would talk about spiders, all the while coupling this with relaxation training. If this was tolerated, the final stage would involve the presentation of the actual feared object. The process is called systematic desensitisation and has been successful in reducing fear. The converse approach, arousing the client's fear so intensely that the person becomes habituated to the onslaught, is called flooding. Implosion therapy would involve the presentation of the feared object at the end of this flooding. A similar process underpins aversion therapy, where a negative reaction to a neutral stimulus is associated with an aversive stimulus (so alcohol might be consumed with an emetic, thereby putting people off the ingestion of alcohol).

Techniques that utilise the principles of operant conditioning involve behaviour modification. For example, token economies might reward appropriate behaviours with rewards (tokens). Modelling will train the person to model their own behaviour on that of a successful other; assertiveness training helps people behave in a socially desirable way.

One of the most widely researched and recently developed behavioural therapies also modifies cognition. Cognitive behavioural therapy (CBT) aims to change a person's maladaptive thoughts, beliefs, perceptions, and behaviour. One way to achieve this is by attribution re-training. Depressed people often attribute their failure to internal causes. Re-training allows the client to focus on their causal attributions more scientifically and rationally and to examine whether they are realistically interpreting their own behaviour and thoughts. A similar model, developed by Albert Ellis in the 1950s, is rational-emotive therapy. This argues that if an event causes a highly emotional reaction (anxiety, depression), it is not the event that has caused the reaction but the person's belief system (you'll recognise echoes here of Lazarus's appraisal model of stress described in the last chapter). Therapy, therefore, challenges these belief systems, showing how a person's way of thinking may be inappropriate. It seems to be particularly effective at reducing general anxiety and unassertiveness.

A therapy that has been interestingly developed in the past few years is 'emotional disclosure'. This is where a person writes about the events or feelings that are causing him or her distress. Studies of Holocaust survivors, the bereaved, and the recently unemployed, for example, have found that this technique reduces the number of trips to the doctor and improves immune system functioning. The outcome for people suffering from serious illness, such as cancer, however, is more mixed. One of the technique's pioneers, James Pennebaker, argues that any benefits that arise are attributable to the changes in cognition that writing brings about. When people write about *why* they are feeling as they are (rather than just describing their feelings), their thoughts become more methodical (and, by extension, less emotional) and this helps their mental health.

Biological treatments

The most commonly administered types of biological treatments are pharmacological and almost every serious mental illness can be treated, in some form, by the use of drugs. There are four general classes of drugs that are used: antipsychotic drugs, antidepressant drugs, anti-manic drugs, and anti-anxiety drugs, some of which are described in the next section.

Mental disorders

As DSM lists hundreds of mental illnesses, it would be impossible to do justice to all of them in the short space here. The next section, therefore, will look at the symptoms and treatment of the most common: schizophrenia, mood disorders, and anxiety disorders. You can find out more about other disorders in the items in the further reading section.

Schizophrenic disorders

Schizophrenia is the most common of the illnesses described as psychosis but it is not unitary: there are different types manifesting different symptoms. In general, the term describes a disorder in which thoughts, perceptions, and emotions are distorted, where bizarre behaviour is common and where the patient is socially withdrawn. Although it translates as 'split mind', it does not mean 'split personality' (that is a different disorder; in schizophrenia, people do not act like, or believe they are, different people). In addition to the behavioural symptoms, individuals may also have cognitive difficulties such as being unable to name many objects beginning with a given letter, and problems with semantic and working memory, and frontal lobe tasks, which has led researchers to conclude that a frontal lobe dysfunction may be responsible for elements of the disorder. Prognosis is very mixed: about a third will never recover and will need to be institutionalised for the rest of their lives, a third will recover and lead normal lives, and a third will recover temporarily only to relapse later.

The disorder is characterised by two categories of symptoms: negative and positive. The positive symptoms include thought disorder – the most pronounced – where a person's thoughts and conversations are disorganised and irrational; delusions, which are beliefs that are contrary to reality, such as believing others are out to get them (delusions of persecution), that they have omnipotent power and control (delusions of grandeur), or that others are controlling them and their thoughts (delusions of control); and hallucinations which are perceptions of stimuli that do not exist or are not present – auditory forms are the most common but they can occur in any modality, including olfactory. Sometimes, the hallucination will involve hearing a running commentary on their life or someone ordering them to act. Negative symptoms are absences of normal behaviour such as emotional expression (flattened affect), social interaction, initiative and persistence, and experiencing pleasure (these can also be absent in other disorders).

DSM-IV describes four subtypes of schizophrenia: undifferentiated, catatonic, paranoid, and disorganised, although these categories are not as clear-cut as they seem; there are some patients who do not fall clearly into any of the subtypes. The undifferentiated type experiences delusions, hallucinations, and disorganised behaviour. The catatonic type (meaning 'to stretch or draw tight') is characterised by motor disturbances such as adopting unusual postures – 'waxy flexibility' describes how a patient's limb may be manipulated and the patient maintains the limb in that position. The paranoid type shows delusions of persecution, grandeur, or control. Finally, the disorganised type is characterised by disturbances of thought. Patients also exhibit inappropriate social behaviour such as laughing at inopportune moments and their conversation is sometimes a word salad, consisting of jumbles of seemingly random words.

The schizophrenias are thought to be caused by genetic, biological, and/or environmental factors, depending on the advocate, although the current evidence points more strongly towards a physical basis. The concordance rate for schizophrenia is higher in identical than fraternal twins, and children whose parents have schizophrenia are more likely to become schizophrenic, even if adopted by non-schizophrenic parents. In terms of brain function, there is evidence that the positive symptoms of schizophrenia are produced by overactivity of dopamine synapses. Chlorpromazine and other antipsychotic drugs used in treatment, for example, inhibit or block the stimulation of dopamine receptors at synapses. These drugs reduce the hallucinations and the amount of incoherent thought. The location of these neurons in schizophrenia is thought to be near the frontal lobe and parts of the limbic system. Neuroimaging research shows that metabolism is decreased in the temporal and frontal cortices and a recent hypothesis holds that the language and thought disturbances in schizophrenia are caused by a failure of localisation of language.

Some of the environmental causes involve the child's relationship with the parent – the parent may accept the child in some ways and reject them in others (leading to 'double-bind'). Families with schizophrenic relatives also appear to be characterised by 'expressed emotion' (EE) – high levels of criticism, hostility, and over-emotionality. Patients from families with low EE tend to recover better than those from high EE families. Accompanying the pharmacological intervention is usually cognitive behavioural therapy (see below), which is designed to help the person with his or her social interactions.

Depression

The most common mood disorder is depression. A diagnosis of major depression is confirmed if a patient shows five DSM-IV symptoms experienced over at least two weeks. These include loss of interest/pleasure in life; intense sadness and despair; loss of concentration; decreased sexual drive and appetite; helplessness; pessimism; fatigue and insomnia. Patients might show suicidal ideation (thinking about killing themselves). Major depression is not a low mood but a serious illness, accurately and painfully reflected in this passage from Lewis Wolpert, Professor of Developmental Biology, in his book about his depression, *Malignant Sadness*:

> It was the worst experience of my life. More terrible even than watching my wife die of cancer. I am ashamed to admit that my depression felt worse than her death but it's true. I was in a state that bears no resemblance to anything I had experienced before. I was not just feeling very low. I was seriously ill. I was totally self-involved, negative and thought about suicide most of the time. I could not think properly let alone work, and wanted to remain curled up in bed all day.

And in this description from Elizabeth Wurtzel's *Prozac Nation*:

> and then, one day, you realise that your entire life is just awful, not worth living, a horror and a black blot on the white terrain of human existence. One morning, you wake up afraid you are going to live ... to all intents and purposes, the deeply depressed are just the walking, waking dead.

An estimated two per cent of the population suffers from depression and the disorder knows no real cultural, social, or economic barriers although it seems to be more prevalent in densely populated urban areas. According to the World Health Organisation, it accounts for 4.4% of the world's disease burden. It tends to be twice as common in women, although this might be because they are more likely to seek help from a GP. Onset is around the mid-twenties, but can occur at any age, and around fifty per cent of patients will experience more than one episode.

One measure used to diagnose the degree of depression is Beck's Depression Inventory which gives respondents scores for statements they chose which best reflect how they feel (e.g. 'I do not feel sad' is scored '0'; ' I am so sad and unhappy that I cannot snap out of it' is scored '3'; the higher the total score, the greater the depression). Aaron Beck also developed a model of depression which utilised a concept called the cognitive triad. This reflected the observation that people felt negative and helpless about the past, the present, and the future (hence, triad) and it has been consistently demonstrated that depressed individuals have a negative attributional style – they will attribute all failure to themselves, rather than to events or situations, and feel that they will fail at anything they attempt in the future. They also develop a sense of what the American psychologist Martin Seligman has described as 'learned helplessness': because they feel trapped and think that nothing they can do will alter anything in their life, depressed individuals will not attempt to change their behaviour. They thus become entangled in an increasingly distressing cycle of helplessness. They also show hopelessness: a catastrophically pessimistic view of the future and their role in it.

Sometimes the cause of this chronic way of feeling and thinking is identifiable. External causes, such as bereavement, unemployment, the end of a relationship, can trigger deep depression. Sometimes, however, the depression appears to have no external cause (as was the case for Lewis Wolpert) and may, therefore, be the result of dysfunctional brain activity.

If a person presents depressive symptoms to a physician, the most likely prescribed treatment for moderate symptoms is regular exercise (this appears to elevate mood, probably via the production of neurotransmitters associated with happiness). The patient might also be prescribed a course of psychological therapy designed to change the way in which the person thinks and behaves. The most common, successful intervention for depression, which is coupled with psychological therapy, is pharmacological. Anti-depressant drugs, such as tricyclic antidepressants, monoamine oxidase inhibitors, and serotonin-specific reuptake inhibitors (SSRIs) such as fluoxetine (Prozac), act by increasing the amount of the neurotransmitter serotonin (and other amines in the case of tricyclics) available to the brain. SSRIs, for example, act by preventing a receptor from removing serotonin from a synapse. When receptors release chemicals, what is left in the synaptic cleft (the space between neurons) is taken back into the releasing cell (a process called re-uptake). The SSRIs appear to prevent this process (although other theories suggest that they act by allowing the brain to reach a threshold of serotonin or that receptors become more receptive to serotonin over time, hence the delay between the ingestion of the drug and the relief from symptoms, which can be weeks).

There is also evidence that depressed individuals show heightened levels of the stress hormones described in the last chapter, especially one called corticotrophin-releasing factor. This leads the brain to release a hormone which prompts the release of cortisol – levels tend to be higher in the morning (when depression is reported to be worse). Patients on medication which increases cortisol can experience depression. Glucocorticoids are also associated with reduced levels of serotonin and with impaired memory, which might explain the lack of concentration.

Usually, a GP will recommend a course of exercise for mild depression (dysthymia) – this is thought to increase the number of amines available (Lewis Wolpert recounts a colleague saying that if you spot someone out jogging, they're probably doing it to keep depression at bay). For more serious forms, exercise is coupled with medication and psychotherapeutic interventions such as CBT. The loss of serotonin plus negative thoughts and feelings are simultaneously addressed. Most depression can be treated in this way but some forms are resistant.

Bipolar disorder

Other patients experience episodes of depression which alternate with episodes of extreme mania – wild, exuberant, unrealistic, disorganised activity and thought ('mania' comes from the Greek for madness). This is bipolar disorder (or 'manic-depression'). Mild versions are called cyclothymic disorder. During the manic phase, speech is rapid and any interruption is met with anger. The person might develop over-blown, fantastical plans for the future that may be abandoned hours or days later. First identified in 1921 by Kraeplin (he called it 'manic-depressive insanity'), the illness can be successfully contained by the drug lithium carbonate but relapse is high. Some battle with the possibility of treatment, fearing that this will sap them of the energy-driven excitement and creativity of the mania. Writing to his future wife, Annabella Milbanke in 1813, the famously tempestuous and temperamentally mercurial Lord Byron admitted:

> You don't like my 'restless' doctrines – I should be very sorry if you did – but I can't stagnate nevertheless – if I must sail let it be on the ocean no matter how stormy – anything but a dull cruise on a level lake.

There are several well-known examples of manic-depression: in recent history, Spike Milligan, Carrie Fisher, Stephen Fry, Richard Dreyfuss, and the late Professor of Psychology at the University of Sussex, Stuart Sutherland, have all suffered from manic-depression, as has the psychologist Kay Jamison who has studied the associations between creativity and manic-depression (her books are highly recommended in the further reading section).

Anxiety disorders

Many disorders in DSM-IV are characterised by a sense of apprehension and doom, accompanied by physical changes such as sweaty palms, tightness in the stomach, and accelerated heart rate, i.e., anxiety. There are various types of anxiety disorder but the most common are generalised anxiety disorder (GAD), phobia (including specific and social phobia), panic disorder, post-traumatic stress disorder (PTSD), and obsessive-compulsive disorder. In general, they are the most widely experienced disorders with one survey noting that they accounted for twenty-seven per cent of primary case patients.

GAD represents an excessive worry about life – work, home, money, relationships – which is experienced daily and over a period of at least six months. The disorder makes individuals restless, irritable, fatigued, and impairs concentration and sleep.

It is the most common anxiety disorder and is often accompanied by depression. One model explains GAD in terms of a failure to meet set and anticipated desirable goals: the need to overcome failure and to anticipate all possible outcomes leads to anxiety. Another holds that this does not explain normal worry and that anxiety serves as an 'alarm function' bringing stimuli that are potentially disturbing into conscious awareness and preparing a person to deal with them. Jeffrey Gray's model argues that anxiety is evoked by punishment, non-reward, and novel stimuli. A behavioural inhibition system (BIS) detects anxiety, helps evaluate it and is represented, neurally, by a complex system of structures and neurotransmitter systems. Yet another model argues that anxiety results from a combination of high trait anxiety and poor coping skills. People with high trait anxiety and those with GAD are supremely sensitive to threat- or anxiety-related stimuli (i.e. they show an attentional bias). Anxious people are more vigilant in detecting threatening than non-threatening faces, and anxiety-related than unrelated words, for example. GAD is commonly treated by sedative anti-anxiety drugs (such as barbiturates or benzodiazepines) called anxiolytics, or by anti-depressants. CBT has also been found to be effective.

Panic disorder has been described as a fear of fear. A person will experience periods of unremitting terror, with increased heart rate and shortness of breath (to such an extent that they misinterpret the signals as meaning they are about to die), sweating, and jelly legs. Onset is usually in young adulthood. In between attacks, they fear another looming (an experience called anticipatory anxiety). The dominant model of panic disorder argues that the anxiety results directly from the type of catastrophic misinterpretation described above and finds that when patients are trained to realize that their physical symptoms do not lead to illness or death, the symptoms recede.

A phobia is a fear of a specific object or event, and named after the Greek god, Phobos (who frightened his enemies). It is often described as irrational because the feared object poses no real threat or harm (although fearing a snake does seem quite rational to anyone not expert in matters ophidian). People have been known to fear the number thirteen (triskaidekaphobia), being alone (monophobia), cats (ailurophobia), even railways (siderophobia). A phobia is only a clinical concern if the fear makes a person's life difficult. Agoraphobia is the most common and is a fear of open spaces (the word *agora* comes from the Greek for market place). It is often associated with panic attacks and can be disabling, with people unable to leave their home.

Social phobia is a fear of being in a situation where a person will be under scrutiny. A large factor in the disorder is concern with how he or she will be perceived: socially phobic people interpret ambiguous feedback negatively. For example, they will report seeing more negative facial expressions in an audience than would someone with no phobia. This misinterpretation leads to further anxiety.

Finally, there are the specific phobias, such as fear of flying (altophobia), heights (acrophobia), enclosed spaces (claustrophobia), spiders (arachnophobia), snakes (ophidiophobia), and so on. Some have argued that the fear of these objects has an evolutionary basis. They argue that the objects we most fear or which disgust us most tend to be either furry or slimy and move quickly and we fear them because we could become contaminated. Another evolutionary theory argues that we fear stimuli that we are evolutionarily prepared to fear because they would harm us if we didn't. Some fears, such as arachnophobia, are extremely difficult to extinguish, possibly because we are genetically prepared to fear an animal that could poison and kill us. This model, clearly, cannot explain why we should fear slugs and snails and perhaps the first model accounts for those. A cross-cultural survey of people's fears undertaken in 1998 found that stimuli could be classed either as fear-relevant, fear-irrelevant, or disgust-relevant. One of the most common treatment approaches is systematic desensitisation, described earlier. More recently, clinicians have developed virtual versions of feared objects and situations to which clients can be exposed. For example, clients might be exposed to virtual spiders or climb on board a virtual plane (if they fear flying). These have met with good success and clients maintain their loss of anxiety at least a year after treatment.

PTSD describes anxiety following a very traumatic event such as a road traffic accident, rape, bank robbery, assault, or natural disaster. Controversially, PTSD has been in the news in the past few years because of the reported increased incidence in servicemen and women returning from wars in the Gulf and Afghanistan and because of a reported exaggeration of PTSD following combat by US troops in Vietnam. Symptoms include re-living the trauma produced by the event – thoughts are intrusive, unpredictable and uncontrollable, avoidant behaviour (denial or feeling emotionally numb), and showing excessive vigilance for stimuli that are trauma-related (a person who has experienced rape, for example, where the rate of PTSD is highest, might be hypervigilant in noticing body movement towards him or her). One model suggests that the disorder occurs because of completion tendency. When the trauma occurs, there is so much information for a person to process that they are unable to cope with it and do not have the means to cope with it (so they might deny it happened or become numb as a means of coping). However, tendency completion keeps the event in mind like an active memory, through flashbacks and hallucinations. Another, more general model suggests that people generally view themselves positively but the event has shattered their belief in the world around them, and has undermined their feeling of invulnerability and their belief that the world is comprehensible and meaningful. Some studies have found that when people write about their trauma and why it feels traumatic (the emotional disclosure technique described earlier on), this reduces the symptoms they feel.

Patients with obsessive-compulsive disorder (OCD) have thoughts that they can't shake off (obsessions) and engage in repetitive behaviours that impede daily life (compulsions). Loss of motor control, constant checking, excessive, ritualised behaviours (such as constant handwashing, showering, grooming), inability to control thoughts, and concerns with contamination are all symptoms. The compulsion is the patient's defence against anxiety caused by the obsessional thoughts but these compulsions become so excessive that they interfere with daily life. Patients do recognise that these behaviours are senseless. The two general types of obsessive thought are a fear of doing something prohibited, and feelings of doubt and uncertainty. For example, patients might fear urinating in church, throwing themselves off a bridge, killing a loved one, swearing in an inappropriate place, and so on, although they rarely engage in these behaviours. The compulsions tend to be of four types: counting, checking, cleaning, and avoidance. Patients might repeatedly check that the cooker is off, might meticulously clean, and fold and refold and refold their clothes.

Some researchers suggest that these behaviours occur to displace unpleasant or painful thoughts. Patients feel that they have to be their best at all times, avoid criticism that they are incompetent, and want to avoid being punished by others for being less than perfect. If painful thoughts become frequent and a way of thinking is devised to combat these, the frequency will lead to an increase in adaptive ways of thinking. Once this habit is formed, the obsessive thoughts might persist, even though the original source of pain no longer exists.

Behavioural therapy has been used to treat OCD – a person might have their hands deliberately dirtied and not be permitted to wash them, for example. Treatment, however, is more successful at combating the compulsions than the obsessions. SSRIs are also used to treat OCD.

Mental ill-health is one of the most pressing medical, psychological, economic, and social problems of our age. The increase in these illnesses may be due to environmental factors (such as increased/decreased wealth, the demands of working, available diet, the way we choose to live) or our increasing sophistication in recognising mental illness as an illness and providing treatment for it. In October 2007, the British government promised to invest around £170 million in 'psychological therapies' for depression and anxiety which, on one level, recognises the seriousness of these illnesses (if only from the economic perspective), and, on another, offers potential help for an enormous number of people.

Coda

In the preface, I cited the quote about a psychologist being someone who goes to the theatre and watches the audience. I noted that this was pithy but mainly wrong. What I hope the material covered in these ten chapters has shown is that although people-watching may be one of the things psychologists do, it isn't the primary one – the discipline actually engages in research that is significantly more rigorous than that. Observation is, of course, important, but psychology is more than a Conan Doyle story.

In the next decade, I suspect we'll see psychologists working more on mental health and its treatment, as the financial and personal burden of these disorders increases. Neuroimaging – and the possibilities it presents – will increase and the designs of its experiments will become more sophisticated and complex. The nature of communication might be the subject of more extensive study, especially given the prevalence of texting, emailing, blogging, chatrooming, and on-line ego-parading. (The 30th editn of ths bk mit evn lk smthin lk ths. :-)) The nature of cultural integration (or lack of it), with the expansion of entities such as the EU and the growth of readily available, cheap flying and the mobility this affords, will be the focus of more research in social psychology. Psychologists already know much about extremism but when I recently spoke to one the Home Office's chief science officers about the people who bombed the London tube on 7 July, he admitted that there was nothing about the behaviour of those individuals on that day that could predict what they did, in the way that they did it. Perhaps this is beyond psychology. It isn't *Cracker*. It isn't *Criminal Minds*.

There is also the faint possibility that, amongst the miasma and lunacy on the internet, the good information it gives so readily will make people better informed (although, as I said to my psychophysiology lab students in the week that Borat was described on the site as being the president of Kazakhstan, avoid Wikipedia).

I hope you enjoyed this mercurial overview. Let me know your impressions: my email address is in the preface.

Right. Must dash. I have to be at the theatre by seven.

(And the audiences are said to be riveting.)

Further reading

Chapter 1

A mass of general psychology texts is available but two highly recommended starting points, which expand on the material here and the rest of the book, are G. Neil Martin, Neil Carlson, and William Buskist's *Psychology*, third edition (2006, Harlow: Pearson Education) and Adrian Furnham's *All in the Mind* (1996, London: Whurr Publishers). David Cohen's *Psychologists on Psychology* (2004, London: Routledge) is an excellent collection of interviews with some influential psychologists. For a good review of the discipline's history, R. Hock's *Forty Studies That Changed Psychology* (2005, Harlow: Pearson Education) and T.H. Leahey's *A History of Psychology*, fifth edition (1997, New Jersey: Prentice Hall International) are worth reading. Finally, two good books on carrying out research in psychology are: R.B. Bausell's *Conducting Meaningful Experiments: 40 Steps to Becoming a Scientist* (1993, London: Routledge) and J. Meltzoff's *Critical Thinking About Research: Psychology and Related Fields* (1998, Washington, DC: American Psychological Association).

Chapter 2

For excellent introductions to biological psychology, see Neil R. Carlson's *Foundations of Physiological Psychology*, sixth edition (2007, Boston: Allyn & Bacon), Fred Toates's *Biological Psychology*, second edition (2007, Harlow: Pearson Education), Stephen Kosslyn *et al.*'s (2002) article, 'Bridging psychology and biology', in *American Psychologist*, 57, 5, 341–351, S.P. Springer and G. Deutsch, *Left Brain, Right Brain*, fifth edition (2001, New York: W.H. Freeman), G. Neil

Martin's *Human Neuropsychology*, second edition (2006, Hemel Hempstead: Prentice Hall Europe) and *Essential Biological Psychology* (2003, London: Arnold). The *Scientific American Mind* series (which appears about four times a year) usually contains excellent summaries about recent behavioural and brain research. Two good books on psychopharmacology are J.A. Hobson's *The Dream Drugstore: Chemically Altered States of Consciousness* (2005, Cambridge, MA: MIT Press) and R.M.A. Julien's brilliant *A Primer of Drug Action*, tenth edition. (2005, San Francisco: W.H. Freeman). A good review of addiction can be found in T.E. Robinson and K.C. Berridge's (2003) article, 'Addiction', in *Annual Review of Psychology*, 54, 25–54. Good reviews of evolutionary psychology can be found in Robin Dunbar *et al.*'s *Evolutionary Psychology* (2005, Oxford: Oneworld), T. Bereczkei's (2000) article, 'Evolutionary psychology: A new perspective in the behavioural sciences', in *European Psychologist*, 5, 3, 175–190; Donald Buss's *Evolutionary Psychology: The New Science of Mind*, second edition (1999, Boston: Allyn and Bacon); and M. Pigliucci's (2006) article, 'Is evolutionary psychology a pseudoscience?', in *Skeptical Inquirer*, 30, 2, 23–4.

Chapter 3

Two general, weighty introductions to sensation and perception are S. Coren *et al.*'s *Sensation and Perception*, sixth edition (2003, Chichester: John Wiley & Sons) and E.B. Goldstein's *Blackwell Handbook of Sensation and Perception* (2004, Oxford: Blackwell). See Vicki Bruce and Andrew Young's *In the Eye of the Beholder* (1998, Oxford: OUP) and G.N. Martin's *Human Neuropsychology* (2006, Pearson Education: Harlow) for more on the neuropsychology of sensation and perception. On facial beauty, see V.S. Johnston's (2006) article, 'Mate choice decisions: The role of facial beauty', in *Trends in Cognitive Sciences*, 10, 1, 10–13. Three excellent readings on consciousness are *The Blackwell Companion to Consciousness* (2006, Oxford: Blackwell), Susan Blackmore's *Conversations on Consciousness: Interviews with Twenty Minds*

(2005, Oxford: Oxford University Press) and her *Consciousness: An Introduction* (2003, London: HodderArnold). An engaging, popular account of the psychology of sleep can be found in Paul Martin's *Counting Sheep* (2002, HarperCollins), and M.R. Nash and G. Benham's (2005) article, 'The truth and hype of hypnosis', in *Scientific American Mind*, 16, 2, 46–53, gives a good review of what we know about hypnosis. For general information on attention, Elizabeth Styles's book, *The Psychology of Attention*, second edition (2002, Hove: The Psychology Press), is a very good start.

Chapter 4

An excellent book on applying learning principles to everyday life, mentioned in the text, is Baldwin and Baldwin's *Behavior Principles in Everyday Life* (1998, Boston: Prentice Hall) and a good review of operant conditioning can be found in J.E.R. Staddon and D.T. Cerutti's (2003) article, 'Operant conditioning', in *Annual Review of Psychology*, 54, 115–144. There are many good books available on memory: Alan Baddeley's *Human Memory: Theory and Practice*, second edition (1996, Hove, UK: The Psychology Press) is one. These articles: R.D. Fields's (2005) 'Making memories stick', in *Scientific American*, February, 74–81, and 'Erasing memories', in *Scientific American*, 16, 4, 28–35; D. Greenberg's (2005) 'Flashbulb memories', in *Skeptic*, 11, 3, 74–80; and M. Gardner's (2006) 'The memory wars, parts 2 and 3', in *Skeptical Inquirer*, 30, 2, 46–50, give excellent, popular accounts of memory acquisition and forgetting. The role of the brain in memory is dealt with well in L.R. Squire and D.L. Schacter's *Neuropsychology of Memory* (2003, Hove, UK: The Psychology Press) and in J.T. Wixted's (2004) article, 'The psychology and neuroscience of forgetting', in *Annual Review of Psychology*, 55, 235–269. Baxendale's 2004 article, 'Memories aren't made of this: amnesia at the movies', in the *British Medical Journal*, 329, 1480–1483, is a brilliant review of how films treat memory loss, and M.D. Kopelman's (2002) article, 'Disorders of memory', in *Brain*, 125, 2152–2190, gives an in-depth review of memory loss.

Chapter 5

Four general, excellent introductions to psycholinguistics and the psychology of language are: Trevor Harley's *The Psychology of Language*, second edition (2002, Hove: Psychology Press), Jean Aitchison's *The Articulate Mammal*, fourth edition (1998, London: Routledge), and Steven Pinker's *The Language Instinct* (1994, London: Penguin) and *Words and Rules* (1999, London: Weidenfeld and Nicholson). A good book on primate language is R. Burling's *The Talking Ape: How Language Evolved* (2005, Oxford: Oxford University Press). On reading development, the following are recommended: P. Fletcher's *Child Language Acquisition* (1998, London: Arnold); A.D. Friederici's (2005) article, 'Neurophysiological markers of early language acquisition: from syllables to sentences', in *Trends in Cognitive Sciences*, 9, 10, 481–488; J.B. Gleason's *The Development of Language*, fourth edition (1997, Boston: Allyn & Bacon); K Rayner *et al.*'s (2002) article, 'How should reading be taught?', in *Scientific American*, March, 71–77. A recent review of what is known about developmental dyslexia can be found in J.-F. Demonet *et al.*'s (2004) article, 'Developmental dyslexia', in N. Brunswick's *Dyslexia: A Beginner's Guide* (forthcoming, Oxford: Oneworld Publications) and *The Lancet*, 363, 1451–1460. Finally, a review of the neural basis of language and language disorders can be found in G. Neil Martin and Nicky Brunswick's chapter in *Human Neuropsychology*, second edition (2006, Harlow: Prentice Hall), and M.A. Gernsbacher and M.P. Kaschak's (2003) article, 'Neuroimaging studies of language production and comprehension', in *Annual Review of Psychology*, 54, 91–114. Sheila Hale's *The Man Who Lost His Language* (2003, London: Penguin) is one of the best personal accounts of the consequences of stroke on language.

Chapter 6

The special issue of *Scientific American* (1998) on *Exploring Intelligence* is a good general introduction to the complex area of intelligence. Two good books on irrational thinking are Stuart Sutherland's *Rationality*

(1992, London: Penguin) and Lewis Wolpert's *Six Impossible Things Before Breakfast* (2006, London: Faber) and a heavyweight consideration of intelligence and reasoning can be found in K. Holyoak and R. Morrison's *The Cambridge Handbook of Thinking and Reasoning* (2005, Cambridge: Cambridge University Press). Two good items on creativity are: K.H. Heilman's *Creativity and the Brain* (2005, Hove: the Psychology Press); and M.A. Runco's (2004) article, 'Creativity', in *Annual Review of Psychology*, 55, 657–687. Sex differences are discussed in L. Cahill's (2005) article, 'His brain, her brain', *Scientific American*, May, 40–47; and Diane Halpern's *Sex Differences in Cognitive Abilities*, third edition (2000, London: Lawrence Erlbaum Associates), and a good item reviewing the role of genes in intelligence is: R. Plomin and J.C. DeFries's (1998) article, 'The genetics of cognitive abilities and disabilities', in *Scientific American*, 287, 5, 40–47. There are many books and articles available on personality and these are some of the best: P.T. Costa and R.R. McCrae's *Personality in Adulthood* (2005, New York: Guilford Press); Walter Mischel's (2004) article, 'Toward an integrative science of the person', in *Annual Review of Psychology*, 55, 1–22; C.F. Monte and R.N. Sollod's *Beneath the Mask*, seventh edition (2002, Chichester: Wiley); L. Pervin's *Current Controversies and Issues in Personality*, third edition (2002, Chichester: Wiley); and G. Matthews *et al.*'s *Personality Traits*, second edition (2003, Cambridge: Cambridge University Press). The role of biology and the brain is well discussed in Turhan Canli's *Biology of Personality and Individual Differences* (2006, Hove: the Psychology Press). For a dissection of Freudian psychodynamic theory, Hans Eysenck's *Decline and Fall of the Freudian Empire* (1985, London: Penguin) can't be bettered.

Chapter 7

The following are some of the best introductions to the psychology of development currently available: H.L. Bee's *The Developing Child*, tenth edition (2004, New York: Addison Wesley Longman); Laura Berk's *Child Development*, seventh edition (2005, Boston: Allyn & Bacon);

L.B. Hendry and M. Kloep's *Lifespan Development: Resources, Challenges and Risks* (2002, London: Thomson Learning); H.R. Schaffer's *Key Concepts in Developmental Psychology* (2006, London: Sage); G. Adams and M. Berzonsky's *The Blackwell Handbook of Adolescence* (2005, Oxford: Blackwell); H.L. Bee and D. Boyd's *Lifespan Development*, fourth edition (2005, New York: Addison Wesley Longman); and Laura Berk's *Development Through the Lifespan*, third edition (2003, Boston: Allyn & Bacon).

Chapter 8

One of the best and entertaining books on social psychology is Elliot Aronson's *The Social Animal*, ninth edition (2003, New York: Worth Freeman). Also recommended is Mike Hogg and Graham Vaughan's *Social Psychology*, fourth edition (2004, Harlow: Pearson Education). Two of the best books on social cognition are S.T. Fiske and S.E. Taylor's *Social Cognition*, second edition (1991, New York: McGraw Hill) and G.B. Moskowitz's *Social Cognition: Understanding Self and Others* (2005, New York: Guilford). For more on groups, see C. Stangor's *Social Groups in Action and Interaction* (2004, New York: Psychology Press); on interpersonal interaction, *The Blackwell Handbook of Social Psychology: Interpersonal Processes* (2001, Oxford: Blackwell); and on influence, Bob Cialdini's classic, *Influence: Science and Practice*, third edition (1993, New York: HarperCollins) and his more recent, popular treatment, *Influence: the Psychology of Persuasion* (2007, New York: HarperCollins).

Chapter 9

Four very good books exploring the psychology of emotion are: Antonio Damasio's *The Feeling of What Happens* (2000, London: Vintage), Keith Oatley and colleagues' *Understanding Emotions* (2006, Oxford: Blackwell), Joseph Le Doux's *Emotional Brain* (2004, New

York: Orion), and Antony Manstead *et al.*'s *Feelings and Emotions* (2004, Cambridge: CUP). Two of the best introductions to health psychology are E.P. Sarafino's *Health Psychology*, sixth edition (2008, Chichester: Wiley) and A.C. Lyons and K. Chamberlain's *Health Psychology* (2006, Cambridge: CUP).

Chapter 10

There are some excellent textbooks on abnormal psychology, written in an accessible way. Four of them are: R.P. Bentall and A.T. Beck's *Madness Explained: Psychosis and Human Nature* (2004, New York: Penguin); R.C. Carson *et al.*'s *Abnormal Psychology and Modern Life*, twelfth edition (2003, New York: HarperCollins); G.C. Davison and J.M. Neale's *Abnormal Psychology*, tenth edition (2006, Chichester: Wiley); and T.F. Oltmans and R.E. Emery's *Abnormal Psychology*, fourth edition (2003, NJ: Prentice Hall). Also completely recommended for their honesty and accuracy are the autobiographical accounts of depression and manic-depression found in Stuart Sutherland's *Breakdown* (1997, London: Weidenfeld), Kay Jamison's *The Unquiet Mind* (1997, London: Picador), and Lewis Wolpert's *Malignant Sadness* (1999, London: Faber). Jamison also considers bipolar disorder and creativity in *Touched With Fire* (1993, New York: Free Press).

Index

A Beginner's Guide to Philosophy of Mind

How do you know that you picked up this book and didn't just dream that you did? Could a computer ever be conscious? Edward Feser takes on one of the most popular fields in modern philosophy and explores the latest ideas about cognitive science, consciousness, and personal identity.

978-1-85168-478-6 | £9.99

"Splendid, the arguments are engaging and provide a refreshing challenge to some of the conventional assumptions in the field."
Charles Taliaferro, Professor of Philosophy, St Olaf College, Minnesota

"A refreshing, provocative, and important addition to the introductory books in philosophy of mind. It should appear on every reading list." **David Oderberg**, Professor of Philosophy, University of Reading

"An excellent way for students to be introduced to the topic."
William Hasker, Professor of Philosophy, Huntington College, Indiana

EDWARD FESER is Visiting Assistant Professor of Philosophy at Loyola Marymount University, California. He has taught and written widely in the areas of philosophy of mind, and his most recent research has focused on new solutions to the mind/body problem.

Browse further titles at
www.oneworld-publications.com

Beginners
GUIDES

A Beginner's Guide to
Oil

World acclaimed scientist Vaclav
Smil reveals everything there is to
know about nature's most
sought-after and controversial
resource from its discovery in the
earth, right through to the political
maelstrom that surrounds it today.

978-1-85168-571-4 | £9.99

"Terrific. Smil has done it again, producing a book from which we
can all create new insights." **Chris Mottershead**, Distinguished
Advisor Energy and the Environment, BP plc, and Director of the
Carbon Trust in London

"Smil's knowledge is famously and fabulously encyclopedic."
Professor Jeffrey D. Sachs, Director, Earth Institute at Columbia
University and author of The End of Poverty: Economic
Possibilities for Our Time

VACLAV SMIL is Distinguished Professor in the Faculty of
Environment at the University of Manitoba, Canada. He is the
author of several books including *Energy: A Beginner's Guide*, also
by Oneworld Publications. He is the first non-American to receive
the American Association for the Advancement of Science Award
for Public Understanding of Science and Technology and is a
Special Fellow of the Royal Society.

Browse further titles at
www.oneworld-publications.com